FATE AND DESTINY

From Holocaust to The State of Israel

FATE AND DESTINY

From Holocaust to The State of Israel

by

Rabbi Joseph B. Soloveitchik

Introduction by

Rabbi Walter Wurzburger

KTAV PUBLISHING HOUSE, INC.

Copyright©1992, 2000
Rabbinical Council of America

Library of Congress Cataloging-in-Publication-Data

Soloveitchik, Joseph Dov.
  [Kol dodi dofek. English]
  Fate and destiny : from Holocaust to the State of Israel / by Joseph B.
Soloveitchik ; introduction by Walter Wurzburger.
    p. cm.
  ISBN 0-88125-685-4
  1. Israel and the diaspora. 2. Jews--United States--Attitudes toward
Israel. 3. Suffering--Religious aspects--Judaism. 4. Covenants--Religious
aspects--Judaism. 5. Jews--Identity. 6. Zionism.   I. Title.

DS132.S6513 2000
296.3'18'09438--dc21

                                                                00-032745

Distributed by
Ktav Publishing House, Inc.
900 Jefferson Street
Hoboken, NJ 07030
201-963-9524 FAX 201-963-0102
Email ktav@compuserve.com

INTRODUCTION

The publication of an English translation of Rabbi Joseph B. Soloveitchik's widely acclaimed essay, *Kol Dodi Dofek*, ("Hark, my beloved knocketh") represents a significant contribution to our understanding of the contemporary Jewish situation. Although the essay is devoted to an analysis of a host of abiding theological issues, such as the problem of evil, the significance of the covenant, and the cause of anti-Semitism, its title was deliberately chosen by Rabbi Soloveitchik as a wake-up alarm to the American Jewish community. He was alerting them to the opportunities presented by the establishment of the State of Israel. The title, taken from Song of Songs (5:2), reflects the worry that we may repeat the tragedy it recounts, when, after anxiously yearning for the return of her lover, the beloved refused to get up from her bed and open the door for him. The Jewish people are urged not to squander opportunities for which they had waited for two thousand years.

Deeply troubled by the failure of the American Jewish community to mobilize its resources against the Holocaust, the Rav, as Rabbi Soloveitchik was reverently called by his numerous devotees, was apprehensive that American Jews might once again fail to properly discharge their historic responsibilities. He feared that, with the entire Arab world arrayed against Israel, and the international community indifferent to the survival of the state, American Jews would not exert themselves enough to secure its safety and well-being.

To rally the Jewish community to intensify its efforts towards this objective, he felt it necessary to call attention to the enormous benefits American Jews had reaped from the state, the miraculous creation of which, especially in the wake of the Holocaust, unmistakably manifests the operation of the hand of God. Without resorting to Messianic categories, Rabbi Soloveitchik convincingly demonstrates the enormous religious significance of the establishment of the state, which serves as a barrier against assimilation and as an incontrovertible refutation of the canard that Jews are damned and doomed.

Because so preeminent a religious authority displayed such enthusiastic support for the state in this essay, it was widely acclaimed in Israel and was reprinted in many anthologies. But its real significance was by no means exhausted by its powerful plea to world Jewry to recognize its debt of gratitude to Israel and to translate it into all-out moral, political, and financial support. It is therefore appropriate now, at a time when the State of Israel is relatively secure and no longer dependent upon the political and financial assistance of the Diaspora, that the English translation of the essay is being published with a new title, *Fate and Destiny*, to reflect more accurately its central theme: the imperative to transform our existence from a causally determined purely natural existence (fate) into an active, meaningful one suffused with a sense of purpose (destiny).

The Rav employs this distinction in discussing the problem of evil He maintains that it is senseless to raise the metaphysical question of why there is evil in the world. The human mind is simply not equipped to tackle this problem. To engage in theodicy is an exercise in futility. Instead of looking for an explanation of our fate—for example, why a particular evil has struck us—we should ask ourselves how we can respond to evil in a manner that will enable us to emerge from this experience as better moral and spiritual beings.

The Rav illustrates his thesis by offering a striking, novel interpretation of the Book of Job. At first, Job desperately searched for an explanation of his bitter fate. But God's speech from the whirlwind made him realize that his task was to utilize the experience of his suffering to become a nobler person. It finally dawned upon him that his much-vaunted piety was a sham, because it was completely egocentric. Learning from his experience, he was transformed into a genuinely pious individual, who understood the need for identification and solidarity with his fellow human beings.

The Rav also invokes distinction between fate and destiny on the collective level to account for the difference between the two Covenants that were established between God and Israel and which form the basis of the uniqueness of the Jew. Thus the texture of Jewish identity is woven of two strands. On the one hand, the pre-Sinaitic Covenant—the "Covenant of Egypt"—affirms that the Jew belongs to a community of fate that encompasses both assimilated and committed Jews. The anti-Semite is not concerned with a Jew's attitude towards Judaism. Jewish distinctiveness is a given, from which there is no escape.

On the other hand, the question of what we make of this unique status as perpetual outsiders—since the days of Abraham the hallmark of our Jewish identity—hinges upon our relationship to the "Sinaitic Covenant," which bids Israel to become a holy people. We must learn to transform our Jewish existence from the realm of sheer fate into a welcome opportunity to mold a meaningful Jewish destiny, least we experience our Jewishness as a terrible burden. As Heinrich Heine expressed it, "Judaism is not a religion but a misfortune." But those who are faithful to the Sinaitic Covenant will rejoice over their ability to participate in the unfolding of the Jewish destiny—helping to overcome evil and usher in an era of true justice, love, and peace.

Yet the Rav insists that the components of Jewishness, the natural, ethnic-national elements as well as the spiritual, ethico-religious ones, are indispensable. One cannot be a religious Jew without a feeling of solidarity and kinship with, and a sense of responsibility for, all Jews, regardless of their degree of religious observance. It was his insistence that Jews formed a community of fate before they were charged at Mount Sinai with becoming a holy people that enabled the Rav to become such an influential voice in opposing the polarization of religious and secular Jewry that imperils the unity of our people.

Walter S. Wurzburger

Kol Dodi Dofek:
It Is the Voice of My Beloved That Knocketh

RABBI JOSEPH B. SOLOVEITCHIK

THE RIGHTEOUS WHO SUFFERS

One of the darkest enigmas with which Judaism has struggled from the very dawn of its existence is the problem of suffering in the world. Already Moses, the master of the prophets, in a moment of mercy and grace, of divine acceptance, pleaded with the Lord that He enlighten him concerning this obscure matter.[1] Moses knocked at the gates of heaven and cried out: "Show me now Thy ways, that I may know Thee, to the end that I may find grace in Thy sight. . . . Show me, I pray Thee, Thy glory" (Exodus 33:13, 18). Why and wherefore do afflictions and pain befall man? Why and wherefore do the righteous suffer and the wicked prosper? From that wondrous morn when Moses, the faithful shepherd, communed with the Creator of the world and sought a comprehensive solution to this question of questions, prophets and sages, through all the generations, have continued to grapple with it. Habakkuk demanded satisfaction

1

for the affront to justice; Jeremiah, King David in his Psalms, and Koheleth pondered this quandary. The entire Book of Job is devoted to this ancient and mysterious query which still agitates and disturbs our world and demands an answer: Why has God allowed evil to reign over His creation?

Judaism, in its strenuous endeavor to reach a safe shore in a world torn asunder by pain and affliction, in its search for an answer to the profound dilemma posed by the evil which—apparently—reigns unboundedly, arrived at a new formulation and definition of the problem, possessed of both depth and breadth. The problem of suffering, Judaism claims, may be raised in two distinct dimensions: fate and destiny. Judaism has always distinguished between an existence of fate and an existence of destiny, between the "I" subject to fate and the "I" endowed with destiny. It is in this distinction that our teaching regarding suffering is to be found.

What is the nature of an existence of fate? It is an existence of compulsion, an existence of the type described by the Mishnah, "Against your will[2] do you live out your life" (Avot 4:29), a purely factual existence, one link in a mechanical chain, devoid of meaning, direction, purpose, but subject to the forces of the environment into which the individual has been cast by providence, without any prior consultation. The "I" of fate has the image of an object. As an object he appears, as made and not as maker. He is fashioned by his passive encounter with an objective, external environment, as one object vis-à-vis another object. The "I" of fate is caught up in a blind, wholly external dynamic. His being is empty, lacking any inwardness, any independence, any selfhood. Indeed, an "I" of fate is a contradiction in terms. For how can "I"-awareness and selfhood coexist with pure externality and objectlike being? It is against this background that the experience of evil arises in all its terror. There are two stages to this fate-laden experience of evil. To begin with, man the object, bound in the chains of an existence of compulsion, stands perplexed and confused before that great mystery—suffering. Fate mocks him; his being, shattered and torn, contradicts itself and negates its own value and worth. The dread of annihilation seizes hold of him and crushes him, both body and soul. The sufferer, quaking and panic-stricken, wanders in the empty spaces of a world upon which the wrath and terror of God weigh heavily. His afflictions appear shadowy and murky, like satanic forces, the offspring of the chaos and the void which pollute the cosmos that had been destined to clearly reflect the image of its Creator. In this stage of perplexity and speechlessness, of confusion of both mind and heart, the sufferer does not pose any questions about the cause and nature of evil. He suffers in silence, groaning under the weight of an agony that has stifled all complaint and suppressed all queries and inquiries.

After this psychic upheaval of the sufferer as the immediate reaction to evil has passed, there follows the intellectual curiosity which endeavors to understand the cosmos and thereby undergird man's confidence and security. In this stage, a person begins to contemplate suffering and to pose grave and difficult questions. He tracks the intellectual foundations of suffering and evil, and seeks to find the harmony and balance between the affirmation and the negation and to blunt the sharp edge of the tension between the thesis—the good—and the antithesis—the bad—in existence. As a result of the question and answer, problem and resolution, he formulates a metaphysics of evil wherewith he is able to reach an accommodation with evil, indeed to cover it up. The sufferer utilizes his capacity for intellectual abstraction, with which he was endowed by his Creator, to the point of self-deception—the denial of the existence of evil in the world.

Judaism, with its realistic approach to man and his place in the world, understood that evil cannot be blurred or camouflaged and that any attempt to downplay the extent of the contradiction and fragmentation to be found in reality will neither endow man with tranquility nor enable him to grasp the existential mystery. Evil is an undeniable fact. There is evil, there is suffering, there are hellish torments in this world. Whoever wishes to delude himself by diverting his attention from the deep fissure in reality, by romanticizing human existence, is nought but a fool and a fantast. It is impossible to overcome the hideousness of evil through philosophico-speculative thought. Therefore, Judaism determined that man, entrapped in the depths of a frozen, fate-laden existence, will seek in vain for the solution to the problem of evil within the framework of speculative thought, for he will never find it. Certainly, the testimony of the Torah that the cosmos is very good is true. However, this affirmation may be made only from the infinite perspective of the Creator. Finite man, with his partial vision, cannot uncover the absolute good in the cosmos. The contradiction in existence stands out clearly and cannot be negated. Evil, which can neither be explained nor comprehended, does exist. Only if man could grasp the world as a whole would he be able to gain a perspective on the essential nature of evil. However, as long as man's apprehension is limited and distorted, as long as he perceives only isolated fragments of the cosmic drama and the mighty epic of history, he remains unable to penetrate into the secret lair of suffering and evil. To what may the matter be compared? To a person gazing at a beautiful rug, a true work of art, one into which an exquisite design has been woven—but looking at it from its reverse side. Can such a viewing give rise to a sublime aesthetic experience? We, alas, view the world from its reverse side. We are, therefore, unable to grasp the all-encompassing framework of being. And it is only within that framework that it is possible to discern the divine plan, the essential nature of the divine actions.

In a word, the "I" of fate asks a theoretical-meta-physical question regarding evil, and this question has no answer. It is insoluble.

In the second dimension of human existence, destiny, the problem of suffering assumes a new form. What is the nature of the existence of destiny? It is an active mode of existence, one wherein man confronts the environment into which he was thrown, possessed of an understanding of his uniqueness, of his special worth, of his freedom, and of his ability to struggle with his external circumstances without forfeiting either his independence or his selfhood. The motto of the "I" of destiny is, "Against your will you are born and against your will you die, but you live of your own free will." Man is born like an object, dies like an object, but possesses the ability to live like a subject, like a creator, an innovator, who can impress his own individual seal upon his life and can extricate himself from a mechanical type of existence and enter into a creative, active mode of being. Man's task in the world, according to Judaism, is to transform fate into destiny; a passive existence into an active existence; an existence of compulsion, perplexity, and muteness into an existence replete with a powerful will, with resourcefulness, daring, and imagination. God's blessing to the work of His hands sums up their entire purpose in life: "Be fruitful and multiply, and fill the earth and subdue it" (Genesis 1:28). Subdue the environment and subject it to your control. If you do not rule over it, it will subjugate you. Destiny bestows upon man a new rank in God's world, it presents him with a royal crown, and man becomes transformed into a partner with the Almighty in the act of creation.

As was stated above, man's existence of destiny gives rise to an original approach to the problem of evil. For so long as a person grapples with the problem of evil while still living an existence of fate, his relationship to this problem expresses itself only in a theoretical-philosophical approach. As a passive creature, the man of fate lacks the strength to struggle with evil in order to contain it or in order to utilize it to achieve an exalted goal.

For the "I" subject to fate is unable to effect any matter of consequence in the sphere of his own existence. He is nourished by his external environment, and his life bears the imprint of that environment. Therefore, he relates to evil from a nonpractical standpoint and philosophizes about it from a purely speculative perspective. He wishes to deny the existence of evil and to create a harmonistic worldview. The end of such an effort can only be complete and total disillusionment. Evil derides the captive of fate and his fantasy about a world which is wholly good and wholly beautiful.

However, in the realm of destiny man recognizes the world as it is and does not wish to use harmonistic formulas in order to gloss over and conceal evil. The man of destiny is highly realistic and does not flinch from confronting evil face to face. His approach is an ethico-halakhic one, devoid of the slightest speculative-metaphysical coloration. When the man of destiny suffers he says to himself: "Evil exists, and I will neither deny it nor camouflage it with vain intellectual gymnastics. I am concerned about evil from a halakhic standpoint, like a person who wishes to know the deed which he shall do; I ask one simple question: What must the sufferer do so that he may live through his suffering?" In this dimension the center of gravity shifts from the causal and teleological aspect of evil (the only difference between causality and teleology being a directional one) to its practical aspect. The problem is now formulated in straightforward halakhic language and revolves about one's daily, quotidian tasks. The fundamental question is: What obligation does suffering impose upon man? This question is greatly beloved by Judaism, and she has placed it at the very center of her world of thought. The halakhah is concerned with this problem as it is concerned with other problems of permitted and forbidden, liability and exemption. We do not inquire about the hidden ways of the Almighty, but, rather, about the path wherein man shall walk when suffering strikes. We ask neither about the cause of evil nor about its purpose, but, rather, about how it might be mended and elevated. How shall a person act in a time of trouble? What ought a man to do so that he not perish in his afflictions?

The halakhic answer to this question is very simple: Afflictions come to elevate a person, to purify and sanctify his spirit, to cleanse and purge it of the dross of superficiality and vulgarity, to refine his soul and to broaden his horizons. In a word, the function of suffering is to mend that which is flawed in an individual's personality. The halakhah teaches us that the sufferer commits a grave sin if he allows his troubles to go to waste and remain without meaning or purpose. Suffering occurs in the world in order to contribute something to man, in order that atonement be made for him, in order to redeem him from corruption, vulgarity, and depravity. From out of its midst the sufferer must arise ennobled and refined, clean and pure. "It is a time of agony unto Jacob, but out of it he shall be saved" (Jeremiah 30:7); i.e., from out of the very midst of the agony itself he will attain eternal salvation. The agony itself will serve to form and shape his character so that he will, thereby, reach a level of exaltedness not possible in a world bereft of suffering. Out of the negation grows the affirmation, out of the antithesis the thesis blossoms forth, and out of the abrogation of reality there emerges a new reality. The Torah itself bears witness to man's powerful spiritual reaction to any trouble that may befall him when it states: "In your distress, when all these things come upon you . . . and you return unto the Lord your God" (Deuteronomy 4:30). Suffering imposes upon man the obligation to return to God in complete and wholehearted repentance.[3] Afflictions are designed to bestir us to repent, and what is repentance if not man's self-renewal and his supernal redemption?

Woe unto the man whose suffering has not precipitated a spiritual crisis in the depths of his being, whose soul remains frozen and lacking forgiveness! Woe unto the sufferer if his heart is not inflamed by the fires of affliction, if his pangs do not kindle the lamp of the Lord that is within him! If a person allows his pains to wander about the vast empty spaces of the cosmos like blind, purposeless forces, then a grave indictment is drawn up against him for having frittered away his suffering.

Judaism has deepened this concept by combining the notion of the mending and elevation of suffering with that of the mending and elevation of divine lovingkindness, divine *ḥesed*. God's acts of *ḥesed*, Judaism declares, are not granted to man as a free gift. Rather, they impose obligations, they make ethico-halakhic demands upon their beneficiary. To be sure, the overflow of divine *ḥesed* derives from God's open, superabundant, and generous hand, but it is not an absolute gift, without conditions or restrictions. The bestowal of good is always to be viewed as a conditional gift—a gift that must be returned—or as a temporary gift. When God endows a person with wealth, influence, and honor, the recipient must know how to use these boons, how to transform these precious gifts into fruitful, creative forces, how to share his joy and prominence with his fellows, how to take the divine *ḥesed* that flows toward him from its infinite, divine source and utilize it to perform, in turn, deeds of *ḥesed* for others. A person who is not brought by divinely bestowed bountiful good to commit himself, absolutely and unreservedly, to God perpetrates a dire sin, and in its wake he finds himself in very difficult straits which serve to remind him of the obligation he owes to God for His gift of *ḥesed*. Our great tannaitic masters have taught us: "A man must pronounce a blessing over evil just as he pronounces a blessing over good" (Berakhot 9:5). In the same way that God's goodness imposes upon man the obligation to perform exalted, sublime deeds, and demands of either the individual or the community original, creative actions, so too do afflictions require of a person that he improve himself, that he purify his life—if he was previously not bestirred to action when God's countenance shined upon him, when God's *ḥesed* overflowed toward him. For there are times when a person is called upon to mend through his afflictions the flaws that he was inflicting upon creation when God "extended peace to him like a river" (cf. Isaiah 66:12). The awareness of the requirement to commit oneself entirely to God and the understanding of one's obligation to purify and sanctify oneself from precisely out of the midst of one's suffering must shine brightly in the soul of a person when he finds himself in the straits and inquires into the meaning of his very existence. At that very moment, he is obliged to mend his unfeeling heart, the moral callousness that caused him to sin while he was yet standing in the great expanses. In a word, man is obliged to resolve not the question of the causal or teleological explanation of suffering in all of its speculative complexity, but rather the question of the rectification of suffering in all of its halakhic simplicity. He does this by transforming fate into destiny, elevating himself from object to subject, from thing to person.

JOB

Consider: This was precisely the answer that the Creator gave to Job. As long as Job philosophized, like a slave of fate, regarding the cause of and reason for suffering, as long as he demanded of God that He reveal to him the nature of evil, as long as he continued to question and complain, asking why and wherefore afflictions befall man, God answered him forcefully and caustically, posing to him the very powerful and pointed question, "Dost thou know?" "Who is this that darkeneth counsel by words without knowledge? Gird up now thy loins like a man; for I will demand of thee, and declare thou unto Me. Where wast thou when I laid the foundations of the earth? Declare, if thou hast the understanding. . . . Dost thou know the time when the wild goats of the rock bring forth? Or

canst thou mark when the hinds do calve?" (Job
38:2–4, 39:1). If you do not even know the ABC of
creation, how can you so arrogantly presume to ask
so many questions regarding the governance of the
cosmos? However, once Job understood how
strange and inappropriate his question was, how
great was his ignorance, once he confessed
unashamedly, "Therefore have I uttered that which
I understood not, things too wonderful for me,
which I knew not" (Job 42:4), the Almighty
revealed to him the true principle contained in suffering, as formulated by the halakhah. God
addressed him as a man of destiny and said: Job, it
is true you will never understand the secret of
"why," you will never comprehend the cause or
telos of suffering. But there is one thing that you *are*
obliged to know: the principle of mending one's
afflictions. If you can elevate yourself via your
afflictions to a rank that you had hitherto not
attained, then know full well that these afflictions
were intended as a means for mending both your
soul and your spirit. Job! when My lovingkindness
overflowed toward you in the manner described
by the verse, "Behold, I will extend peace to her
like a river" (Isaiah 66:12), when you were a promi-
nent and influential person—"And this man [Job]
was the greatest of all the people of the East" (Job
1:3)—you did not fulfill the task that My abundant
lovingkindness imposed upon you. True, you were
a wholehearted and upright man, you feared God
and shunned evil; you did not use your power or
wealth for bad; you dispensed a great deal of charity—"I put on righteousness, and it clothed itself
with me: my justice was as a robe and a diadem"

(Job 29:14)—nor were you ever loath to extend your help and support to the needy, but you came to their aid in times of distress—"For I delivered the poor that cried, the fatherless also, that had none to help him" (Job 29:12). However, in two respects you were lacking in that great attribute of *ḥesed*, of lovingkindness: (1) You never assumed your proper share of the burdens of communal responsibility and never joined in the community's pain and anguish; (2) nor did you ever properly empathize with the agonies of the individual sufferer. As a kind, good-hearted person, you took momentary pity on the orphan, you were very wealthy and could afford to give substantial charitable contributions without straining your financial resources. However, *ḥesed* means more than a passing sentiment, a superficial feeling; *ḥesed* demands more than a momentary tear or a cold coin. *Ḥesed* means to merge with the other person, to identify with his pain, to feel responsible for his fate. And this attribute of *ḥesed* you lacked in your relationships with the community and with the individual.

You were a contemporary of Jacob, who struggled with Laban, with Esau, and with the man at the ford of the Jabbok.[4] Did you seek to help him and offer him of your counsel and wisdom? Who was Jacob? A poor shepherd. And you? A wealthy and influential man. Had you accorded Jacob a proper measure of sympathy, of caring, had you treated him with the attribute of steadfast lovingkindness, then he would not have had to endure so much suffering. You lived during the time of Moses and were numbered among Pharaoh's advisers. Did you lift a finger when Pharaoh decreed, "Every son that is born shall ye cast into the river", (Exodus 1:22), when the taskmasters worked your brethren with rigor? You were silent and did not protest, for you were afraid to be identified with the wretched slaves. To slip them a coin—fine, but to intervene publicly on their behalf—out of the question. You were fearful lest you be accused of dual loyalty. You were active during the generation of Ezra and Nehemiah and those who went up with them from Babylon. You, Job, with your wealth and influence, could have significantly accelerated the process of *yishuv haarez*, of settling the land of Israel and building the Temple. However, you were deaf to the historical cry of the people. You did not storm and protest against the Sanballats, the Samaritans, and the other Jew-haters who sought to destroy the small Jewish community in Judea and thereby extinguish the last glimmer of hope of God's people. What did you do when those who went up from Babylon cried out, from the depths of pain and despair, "The strength of the bearers of burdens is decayed, and there is much rubbish; so that we are not able to build the wall" (Nehemiah 4:4)? You stood by idly! You did not participate in the struggle and suffering of those who fought for Judaism, for the land of Israel, and for the redemption; you never offered a single sacrifice on their behalf. You were concerned only about your own welfare, you would pray and offer a burnt-offering only on your own behalf. "And it was so, when the days of their [Job's sons'] feasting were gone about, that Job sent and sanctified them, and rose up early in the morning, and offered burnt-offerings according to the

number of them all; for Job said: It may be that my
sons have sinned, and blasphemed God in their
hearts" (Job 1:5). Did you ever once offer a prayer
on behalf of a stranger in a spirit of sharing in his
grief? No! Don't you know, Job, that prayer is the
possession of the community as a whole, and that
an individual cannot approach the King and
appeal to Him and present his requests before Him
unless he redeems himself from his isolation and
seclusion and attaches himself to the community?
Have you forgotten that Jewish prayer is recited in
the plural—"a man should always associate himself with the congregation" (Berakhot 30a), that
Jewish prayer means that one soul is bound up
with another soul, that stormy and tempestuous
hearts merge and blend? You did not know how to
utilize the formulation of prayer in the plural as
fixed by the nation in order to include yourself
among the many and in order to bear the yoke of
your fellowman. Job, if you but wish to learn the
teaching of the mending of one's afflictions, you
must first apprehend the secret of prayer that
brings the "I" closer to his fellow, you must first be
able to recite clearly the authentic text of prayer
whereby the individual partakes of the experience
of the many, and you must first understand the
idea of ḥesed as it is embodied by the prayerful person who rises above his individual uniqueness to
achieve a sense of communal unity. You cannot
discharge your obligation by merely dispensing a
few clattering coins from amidst the abundant
wealth with which you have been blessed. Only
through a prayer fraught with the experience of a
shared communal suffering will you be redeemed.

You did not understand the teaching contained in lovingkindness, and you frittered away the blessing which I bestowed upon you. Now seek to apprehend the teaching contained in suffering. Perhaps now you will be able to mend, in pain and grief, the sinful behavior you indulged in while in your previous state of self-satisfaction and pseudo-happiness.

God addressed the friends of Job: "Now therefore, take unto you seven bullocks and seven rams, and go unto My servant Job, and offer up for yourselves a burnt-offering; and My servant Job shall pray for You" (Job 42:8). Behold, I will test Job yet again. Let him be scrutinized publicly; will he now know how to pray for his fellowman, how to share in his suffering? Has he learned anything in this hour of calamity and wrath? Has he properly appropriated a new formulation of prayer which includes and encompasses the community? If he pleads on your behalf, then both he and you will be redeemed, "for him I will accept" (Job 42:8). Then you will know that Job has been delivered from the straits of egoism and has entered into the wide expanses of sympathy with the community and solidarity with one's fellowman, that his sense of detachment has disappeared and in its place a true spirit of communion has emerged. The great miracle occurred. Job suddenly grasped the true nature of Jewish prayer. In a moment he discovered its plural form, he described the attribute of ḥesed which sweeps the individual from the private to the public domain. He began to live the life of the community, to feel its griefs, to mourn over its calamities, and to rejoice in its happiness. The afflictions of Job found their true rectification when he extricated himself from his fenced-in confines, and the divine wrath abated. "And the Lord turned the captivity of Job, *when he prayed for his friends*" (Job 42:10).

MISSING THE MOMENT

Now, as well, we are living in troubled times, in days of wrath and distress. We have been the victims of vicious attacks; we have been stricken with suffering. During the last fifteen years we have been afflicted with torments which are unparalleled in the thousands of years of exile, oppression, and religious persecution. This era of suffering, this dark chapter in our history, did not come to an end with the establishment of the State of Israel. Even now, today, the State of Israel still finds itself in a crisis situation, fraught with danger, and we are all filled with fear and trembling regarding the fate of the *Yishuv*, of the struggling Jewish community in the land of Israel. We are witnesses to the rising star of the wicked and the international perversion of justice deriving from the indifference to the principles of righteousness and equity exhibited by the states of the West. Everyone flatters our enemies and adversaries, they all grovel before them in a display of hypocrisy and sycophancy of the worst order. Everyone seeks their well-being, while they treat our beleaguered and fragile *Yishuv* in the same manner as that wealthy man who stole the little ewe lamb from his poor, weak, and helpless neighbor.

The well-known metaphysical problem arises yet again and the sufferer asks: "Why dost Thou show me iniquity and beholdest mischief? . . . For the wicked doth beset the righteous; therefore, right goes forth perverted" (Habakkuk 1 :3–4). However, as we emphasized earlier, God does not address Himself to this question, and man receives no reply concerning it. The question remains obscure and sealed, outside the domain of logical thought. For "Thou canst not see My face, for man shall not see Me and live" (Exodus 33:20). When the impulse of intellectual curiosity seizes hold of a person, he ought to do naught but find strength and encouragement in his faith in the Creator, vindicate God's judgment, and acknowledge the perfection of His work. "The Rock, His work is perfect; for all His ways are justice" (Deuteronomy 32:4). If we wish to probe deeply, to question profoundly during a period of nightmarish terrors, then we have to pose the question in a halakhic form and ask: What is the obligation incumbent upon the sufferer deriving from the suffering itself? What commanding voice, what normative principle arises out of the afflictions themselves? Such a question, as we stated above, has an answer which finds its expression in a clear halakhic ruling. We need not engage in metaphysical speculation in order to clarify the law of the rectification of evil. "It is not in heaven" (Deuteronomy 30:12). If we should succeed in formulating this teaching without getting involved in the question of cause and telos, then we will attain complete redemption, and the biblical promise, "Take counsel together and it shall be brought to naught; speak the word and it shall not stand; for God is with us" (Isaiah 8:10), shall be fulfilled with regard to us. Then, and only then, will we rise from the depths of the Holocaust, possessed of a heightened spiritual stature and adorned with an even more resplendent historical grandeur, as it is written: "Also the Lord gave Job twice as much as he had before" (Job 42:10)—double, both in quantity and in quality.

The teaching of the rectification of suffering—when it is put into practice—demands of the sufferer both courage and discipline. He must find within himself and draw upon prodigious resources, and subject himself to a rigorous self-examination and self-evaluation, untainted by the slightest hint of partiality or self-indulgence; he must contemplate his past and envisage his future with complete and unwavering honesty. It was not easy for Job to mend his suffering. And we as well, faint-hearted and weak-willed as we are, bound in the chains of fate and lacking personal fortitude, are now called upon by divine providence to clothe ourselves in a new spirit, to elevate ourselves to the rank of the rectification of our afflictions, afflictions which are demanding of us that we provide them with their deliverance and redemption. For this purpose, we need to examine our own reflection with spiritual heroism and total objectivity. This reflection breaks through both past and present together in order to confront us directly.

If the gracious divine bounties which have been showered upon both the individual and the community obligate their beneficiary to perform special, concrete deeds, even if these bounties (like wealth, honor, influence, power, and the like,

which are acquired through exhausting labor) have
been bestowed upon man in a natural manner, how
much more so do the divine bounties which are
bequeathed in a supernatural manner, in the form
of a miracle which takes place outside the context
of the basic lawfulness governing the concatena-
tion of historical events, bind the miracle's beneficiary to God. God's miraculous boon of *ḥesed*
imposes upon man the absolute obligation to fulfill
the great commandment which cries out from the
very midst of the miracle itself. A transcendental
commandment always accompanies a miraculous
act—"Command the Israelites!" Woe unto the beneficiary of a miracle if he does not recognize the
miracle performed on his behalf, if he is deaf to the
imperative which echoes forth from the metahis-
torical event. How unfortunate is he who has
enjoyed God's wonders if the spark of faith has not
been kindled within him, if his conscience does not
tremble and take heed at the sight of the extraordi-
nary occurrence.

When a miracle does not find its proper answering echo in the form of concrete deeds, an exalted
vision degenerates and dissipates, and the divine
attribute of justice begins to denounce the ungrate-
ful beneficiary of the miracle. "The Almighty
sought to make Hezekiah the Messiah, and
Sennacherib, Gog and Magog. The attribute of justice objected, 'You performed all these miracles on
behalf of Hezekiah, yet he did not utter song before
You. Shall You, then, make him the Messiah ?'"[5]
Then come times of distress; the hour of suffering
makes its appearance. Suffering is the last warning
wherewith divine providence alerts the man lack-

ing any sense of appreciation for the good he has received. One must respond to this last pronouncement, arising out of suffering, with alacrity, and must answer the voice of God calling out to man, "Where art thou!" Judaism has always been very strict regarding the prohibition against missing the moment. It possesses a highly developed and sensitive time-consciousness and views the slightest delay as a sin. There are occasions when a person can lose his entire world on account of one sin— "and he lingered." What is the prohibition against overdue sacrifices (*notar*) if not a matter of being late? In what does the grave sin of the profanation of the Sabbath consist if not in the performance of work one moment after sunset, the very same work that had been permitted one moment before sunset? Does not the culpable nonfulfillment of commandments often take the form of lingering for but a few minutes: for example, reciting the *Shema* after its set time has elapsed, taking the *lulav* after sundown, and the like. Two kings of Israel, anointed of God and national heroes, sinned, repented fully, and confessed. The sin of one was not pardoned right away, while God reconciled Himself to the other and forgave him the very moment he confessed. God treated Saul in accordance with the attribute of strict justice and tore his kingdom away from him. However, with regard to David, God tempered justice with mercy, and He did not deprive David's descendants of the Davidic kingship. Why did God treat Saul with such severity and act so graciously toward David? But the question is not a particularly difficult question! The answer is very simple. David did not miss the

opportune moment and confessed his sin immediately. Saul lingered just a bit, and because of this
delay his kingdom was taken away from him.
When Nathan the prophet came to David and
exclaimed, "Thou art the man!" (2 Samuel 12:7),
David started to confess immediately and did not
put off his plea to God for even the slightest
moment. "And David said unto Nathan: I have
sinned against the Lord" (2 Samuel 12:13). Saul
squandered that precious, inestimable moment.
After he heard Samuel's rebuke—"Wherefore then
didst thou not hearken to the voice of the Lord, but
didst fly upon the spoil?" (1 Samuel 15:19)—he
began to argue with Samuel prior to confessing.
"And Saul said unto Samuel: Yea, I have hearkened
to the voice of the Lord, and have gone the way
which the Lord sent me" (1 Samuel 15:20). It is true
that in the very same encounter with Samuel, Saul
confessed his sin, broken-hearted and contrite.
"And Saul said unto Samuel: I have sinned; for I
have transgressed the commandment of the Lord
and thy words" (1 Samuel 15:24). But his confession was not forthcoming at the desired moment,
and this slight delay brought about the loss of his
kingdom. By the time he confessed, the decree had
already been sealed and his situation was irreme-
diable. "The Lord hath torn the kingdom of Israel
from thee this day" (1 Samuel 15:28). Had Saul not
missed the right moment, had he not tarried, then
his kingdom would have endured.[6]

What is the gist of the Song of Songs if not the
description of the tragic and paradoxical delay of
the Shulammite maiden, drunk with love and over-
whelmed with yearning, when a favorable

moment, replete with awe and majesty, beckoned to her—if not her missing that great, exalted, and momentous opportunity that she had dreamed about, fought for, and sought so passionately? The tender and delicate Shulammite maiden, impelled by longing for her bright-eyed beloved, roamed during sun-drenched days through the bypaths of vineyards and over the crests of mountains, through fields and gardens, and during pale, magical moonlit nights, during pitch-black nights, between the walls, searching for her beloved. One cold and rainy night she returned to her tent, tired and worn-out, and fell fast asleep. The sound of quick and light footsteps could be heard in the silence of the tent. On that strange and mysterious night, suddenly the beloved emerged from out of the dark and knocked on the door of his darling, who had intensely yearned for and awaited him. He knocked and pleaded with her to open the door of her tent. "It is the voice of my beloved that knocketh. 'Open to me, my sister, my darling, my dove, my undefiled; for my head is filled with dew, my locks with the drops of the night'" (Song of Songs 5:2). The great moment that she had looked forward to with such impatience and longing materialized unexpectedly. Her elusive, self-concealing beloved, tired of wandering and hardships, appeared with his curly hair, black eyes, powerful build, and radiant countenance. He stood by her door, stretched his hand in through the hole in the latch, sought refuge from the damp of night, and wished to tell her about his powerful love, about his desires and yearnings, about a life of companionship, filled with delight and joy, about the real-

ization and attainment of their aspirations and
hopes. Only the slight movement of stretching out
her hand and turning the latch intervened between
her and her beloved, between the great dream and
its complete fulfillment. With a single leap the
Shulammite maiden could have obtained her
heart's longings—"Draw me, we will run after thee
. . . we will be glad and rejoice in thee" (Song of
Songs 1:4). But the heart is deceitful, and who can
discern it? Precisely on that very night, a strange,
stubborn indolence overcame her. For a brief
moment the fire of longing that had burned so
brightly was dimmed, the fierce passion ebbed, her
emotions were stilled, her dreams, extinguished.
The maiden refused to descend from her bed. She
did not open the door of the tent to her handsome
beloved. A cruel madness swept her into an abyss
of oblivion and indifference. The maiden proved
stubborn and lazy and rained down a multitude of
excuses and rationalizations to account for her
peculiar behavior: "I have put off my coat; how
shall I put it on? I have washed my feet; how shall
I soil them?" (Song of Songs 5:3). The beloved
knocked again and again, and the more insistent
his knocks, the louder they grew, the more her icy,
defiling madness increased in intensity. As the
whispered entreaties of the beloved pierced the
silence of the night, the heart of his darling became
harder and harder—like stone. The beloved continued to knock, pleading patiently, and together with
his knocks the clock sounded the minutes and
hours. The maiden paid no heed to the voice of her
beloved; the door to her tent remained shut up
tight. The moment was lost; and the vision of an

exalted life faded away. It is true that after a brief delay the maiden awoke from her slumber and, confused and startled, leapt from her bed to welcome her beloved: "I rose up to open to my beloved" (Song of Songs 5:5); but she arose too late. Her beloved had stopped knocking and vanished into the darkness of the night—"My beloved had turned away and gone" (Song of Songs 5:6). Her life's joy was fled; her existence—a desolate wilderness, an empty waste. The saga of her passionate quest began anew. She is still wandering amidst the shepherds' tents—searching for her beloved.

SIX KNOCKS

Eight years ago, in the midst of a night of terror filled with the horrors of Maidanek, Treblinka, and Buchenwald, in a night of gas chambers and crematoria, in a night of absolute divine self-concealment (hester panim muḥlat), in a night ruled by the satan of doubt and apostasy which sought to sweep the maiden from her house into the Christian church, in a night of continuous searching, of questing for the Beloved—in that very night the Beloved appeared. "God who conceals Himself in His dazzling hiddenness" suddenly manifested Himself and began to knock at the tent of His despondent and disconsolate love, twisting convulsively on her bed, suffering the pains of hell. *As a result of the knocks on the door of the maiden, wrapped in mourning, the State of Israel was born!*
How many times did the Beloved knock on the door of the tent of His love? It appears to me that we can count at least six knocks.

First, the knock of the Beloved was heard in the political arena. No one can deny that from the standpoint of international relations, *the establishment of the State of Israel, in a political sense, was an almost supernatural occurrence.* Both Russia and the Western countries jointly supported the idea of the establishment of the State. This was perhaps the only proposal where East and West were united. I am inclined to believe that the United Nations organization was created specifically for this purpose—in order to carry out the mission which divine providence had set for it. It seems to me that one cannot point to any other concrete achievement on the part of the U.N. Our sages, of blessed memory, already expressed the view that at times "rain" descends "for a single person," or for a single blade of grass. I do not know whom the journalists, with their eyes of flesh and blood, saw sitting in the chairman's seat during that fateful session when the General Assembly decided in favor of the establishment of the State. However, someone who at that time observed matters well with his spiritual eye could have sensed the presence of the true chairman who presided over the discussion—i.e., the Beloved! It was He who knocked with His gavel on the podium. Do we not interpret the verse "That night the sleep of the king fled" (Esther 6:1) as referring to "the sleep of the King of the universe" (Megillah 15b). Were it Ahasuerus alone who could not sleep, it would have been of no consequence, and the salvation of Israel would not have blossomed forth on that night. However, if it is the King of the universe Who, as it were, does not slumber, then the redemption will be born. If it had been John Doe who called the session of the United Nations to order, the State of Israel would never have come into being—but if the Beloved knocked on the chairman's podium, then the miracle occurred. It is the voice of my Beloved that knocketh!

Second, the knocking of the Beloved could be heard on the battlefield. *The small Israeli Defense Forces defeated the mighty armies of the Arab countries.* The miracle of "the many in the hands of the few" took place before our very eyes. And an even greater miracle occurred at that time. God hardened the heart of Ishmael and enjoined him to do battle against the State of Israel. Had the Arabs not declared war against the State, and, instead, agreed to the Partition Plan, the State of Israel would have lacked Jerusalem, a large part of the Galilee, and several areas of the Negev. Had Pharaoh, thousands of years ago, allowed the Israelites to depart from Egypt immediately, in accordance with Moses' original request, Moses would have been bound to keep his promise and would have had to return after three days. However, Pharaoh hardened his heart and did not hearken to Moses. The Almighty took the Israelites out of Egypt with a strong hand and an outstretched arm. Consequently, Moses' pledge that they would return to Egypt was no longer binding. A bilateral contract cannot bind one party if the other party refuses to fulfill his obligations. It is the voice of my Beloved that knocketh!

Third, the Beloved began to knock as well on the door of the theological tent, and it may very well be that this is the strongest knock of all. I have often

emphasized, when speaking of the land of Israel,
that all the claims of Christian theologians that God
deprived the Jewish people of its rights in the land
of Israel, and that all the biblical promises regarding Zion and Jerusalem refer, in an allegorical
sense, to Christianity and the Christian church,
*have been publicly refuted by the establishment of the
State of Israel and have been exposed as falsehoods*, lacking all validity. It requires a comprehensive knowledge of Christian theological literature, from Justin
Martyr down to contemporary theologians, to
properly appreciate the great miracle which so
clearly invalidated this central premise of Christian
theology. We ought to take note of the "learned"
explanation of our Secretary of State, Mr. [John
Foster] Dulles, who also serves as an elder in the
Episcopal Church, at a meeting of a Senate com-
mittee, that the Arabs hate the Jews because the
Jews killed the founder of their religion. This
"explanation" possesses profound, hidden symbolic significance. I am not a psychologist and certainly not a psychoanalyst; however, I do have some
acquaintance with the Talmud, and I remember
well what our sages said about Balaam: "From his
blessing . . . you may learn what was in his heart"
(Sanhedrin 105b; cf. Rashi on Numbers 24:6). When
a person speaks at length, the truth may, at times,
slip out. When one of the senators asked the
Secretary of State: "Why do the Arabs hate the
Jews?" he really wanted to reply: "I myself, as a
Christian, don't bear any great love for them, for
they killed our Messiah and, as a result, lost their
share in the inheritance of Abraham." However, an
angel intervened or a bit was placed in the

Secretary's mouth (as happened to Balaam, according to the Sages' interpretation of the verse "and
He put a word into his mouth" [Numbers 23:16; cf.
Rashi ad loc. and Sanhedrin 105b), and instead of
uttering the words "our Messiah" and "I myself,"
alternative terms slipped out of his mouth, and he
said "the Arabs" and "Muhammad." In his sub-
conscious he is afraid of the "terrible" fact that the
Jewish people rule over Zion and Jerusalem. I find
special pleasure in reading articles about the State
of Israel in Catholic and Protestant newspapers.
Against their will they have to use the name
"Israel" when they report the news about Zion and
Jerusalem which are now in our hands. I always
derive a particular sense of satisfaction from reading in a newspaper that the response of the State of
Israel is not as yet known, since today is the
Sabbath and the offices of the ministries are closed,
or from reading a news release from the United
Press on Passover eve that "the Jews will sit down
tonight at the Seder table confident that the mira-
cles of Egypt will recur today." It is the voice of my
Beloved that knocketh!

Fourth, the Beloved is knocking in the hearts of
the perplexed and assimilated youths. The era of
self-concealment (*hastarat panim*) at the beginning
of the 1940s resulted in great confusion among the
Jewish masses and, in particular, among the Jewish
youth. Assimilation grew and became more ram-
pant, and the impulse to flee from Judaism and
from the Jewish people reached a new height. Fear,
despair, and sheer ignorance caused many to spurn
the Jewish community and board the ship "to flee
unto Tarshish from the presence of the Lord"

(Jonah 1:3). A raging, seemingly uncontrollable, torrent threatened to destroy us. Suddenly, the Beloved began to knock on the doors of the hearts of the perplexed, and *His knock, the rise of the State of Israel*, at the very least slowed the process of flight. Many of those who, in the past, were alienated from the Jewish people are now tied to the Jewish state by a sense of pride in its outstanding achievements. Many American Jews who had been semi-, demi-, or hemi-assimilated are now filled with fear and concern about the crisis overtaking the State of Israel, and they pray for its security and welfare, even though they are still far from being completely committed to it. Even those who are opposed to the State of Israel—and there are such Jews—are compelled to defend themselves, without letup, against the strange charge of dual loyalty, and they loudly proclaim, day in day out, that they have no share in the Holy Land. It is good for a Jew not to be able to hide from his Jewishness, but to be compelled to keep on answering the question "Who art thou? And what is thine occupation?" (cf. Jonah 1:8), even if, overcome by cowardice, he lacks the strength and courage to answer proudly: "I am a Hebrew; and I fear the Lord, the God of heaven" (Jonah 1:9). This persistent question, "Who art thou?" binds him to the Jewish people. The very fact that people are always talking about Israel serves to remind the Jew in flight that he cannot run away from the Jewish community with which he has been intertwined from birth. Wherever we turn we encounter the word "Israel"; whether we listen to the radio, read the newspaper, participate in symposia about current affairs, we find the question of Israel always being publicly discussed.

This fact is of particular importance for Jews who are afflicted with self-hatred and wish to escape from Judaism and flee for their lives. They, like Jonah, seek to hide in the innermost part of the ship and wish to slumber, but the shipmaster does not allow them to ignore their fate. The shadow of Israel pursues them unceasingly. Buried, hidden thoughts and paradoxical reflections emerge from the depths of the souls of even the most avowed assimilationists. And once a Jew begins to think and contemplate, once his sleep is disturbed—who knows where his thoughts will take him, what form of expression his doubts and queries will assume? It is the voice of my Beloved that knocketh!

The fifth knock of the Beloved is perhaps the most important of all. For the first time in the history of our exile, divine providence has surprised our enemies with the sensational discovery that *Jewish blood is not free for the taking, is not* hefker! If anti-Semites wish to describe this phenomenon as "an eye for an eye," so be it; we will agree with them. If we wish to heroically defend our national-historical existence, we must, at times, interpret the verse "an eye for an eye" (Exodus 21:24) literally. How many eyes did we lose during the course of our bitter exile because we did *not* return blow for blow. The time has come for us to fulfill the law of "an eye for an eye" in its plain, simple sense. I am certain that everyone who knows me knows that I am a believer in the Oral Law and, consequently, that I do not doubt that the verse refers to monetary compensation, in accordance with the halakhic interpretation. However, with regard to Nasser or the Mufti I would demand that we interpret the phrase "an eye for an eye" in a strictly literal sense—as referring to the removal of the concrete, actual eye. Pay no attention to the fine phrases of well-known Jewish assimilationists or socialists, who continue to adhere to their outworn ideologies and think that they are living in the Bialystok, Minsk, or Brisk of 1905, and who publicly declaim that it is forbidden for Jews to take revenge at any time, any place, and under all circumstances. Vanity of vanities! Revenge is forbidden when it serves no purpose. However, if by taking revenge we raise ourselves up to the plane of self-defense, then it becomes the elementary right of man qua man to avenge the wrongs inflicted upon him.

The Torah has always taught us that a person is permitted, indeed, that it is his sacred obligation, to defend himself. The biblical law about the thief breaking into a house (Exodus 22:1–2) indicates that it is a firmly fixed halakhic principle that a person is permitted to defend not only his life but also his property.[7] If the thief who comes to steal the money of the householder is capable of murdering the householder if he does not accede to his demands, then the householder is permitted to rise up against the lawbreaker and kill him. It is not for naught that the Torah informs us that its two great heroes, Abraham and Moses, both took up arms in order to defend their brethren—"and he [Abraham] armed his trained men" (Genesis 14:14; and cf. Rashi ad loc.); "and he [Moses] smote the Egyptian" (Exodus 2:12). Such behavior does not contradict the principles of mercy and lovingkindness. On the contrary, a passive attitude, renouncing self-defense, is likely, at times, to give rise to the worst types of cruelty. "And I will get Me honor through Pharaoh and through all his hosts; and the Egyptians shall know that I am the Lord" (Exodus 14:4). God did not seek honor and fame; He wanted Pharaoh, Moses' contemporary, to know that he would have to pay a high price for the decree, "Every son that is born ye shall cast into the river" (Exodus 1:22). And now, as well, it is God's wish that the blood of the Jewish children who were murdered while reciting the *Shemoneh 'Esreh* be avenged. When God smote Egypt, He wished thereby to demonstrate that Jewish blood always has claimants. Today, also, it is necessary to convince not only the current Egyptian tyrant but also the self-declared saint, Nehru, the British Foreign Office, and the "moralists" in the United Nations that Jewish blood is not ownerless. Therefore, how grotesque is the attempt to convince us that we ought to rely on the declaration of the three great powers guaranteeing the status quo. We all know from experience how much value there is to the promises of the British Foreign Office and to the "friendship" of certain well-known officials in our own State Department. And, in general, how absurd it is to demand of a people that it be completely dependent upon the good graces of others and that it relinquish the ability to defend itself. The honor of every community, like the honor of every individual, resides in the ability to defend its existence and honor. A people that cannot ensure its own freedom and security is not truly independent. The third phrase in God's promise of redemption is: "And I will redeem you with an outstretched arm *and with great judgments*" (Exodus 6:7). *Blessed be He Who has granted us life and brought us to this era when Jews have the power, with the help of God, to defend themselves!*

Let us not forget that the venom of Hitlerian anti-Semitism, which made the Jews like the fish of the sea to be preyed upon by all, still infects many in our generation who viewed the horrific spectacle of the gassing of millions with indifference, as an ordinary event not requiring a moment's thought. The antidote to this deadly poison that envenomed minds and benumbed hearts is the readiness of the State of Israel to defend the lives of its sons, its builders. It is the voice of my Beloved that knocketh!

The sixth knock, which we must not ignore, was heard when the gates of the land were opened. A Jew who flees from a hostile country now knows that he can find a secure refuge in the land of his ancestors. This is a new phenomenon in our history. Until now, whenever Jewish communities were expelled from their lands, they had to wander in the wilderness of the nations and were not able to find shelter in another land. Because the gates were barred before exiles and wanderers, many Jewish communities were decimated. Now the situation has changed. If a particular people expels the Jewish minority from its midst, the exiles can direct their steps unto Zion, and she, like a compassionate mother, will gather in her children. We have all been witness to Oriental Jewry's settling in the land of Israel in the past few years. Who knows what might have befallen our brethren in the lands in which they had settled had not the land of Israel brought them by boats and planes to her? Had the State of Israel arisen before Hitler's Holocaust, hundreds of thousands of Jews might have been saved from the gas chambers and crematoria. The miracle of the State came just a bit late, and as a result of this delay thousands and tens of thousands of Jews were murdered. However, now that the era of divine self-concealment (*hester panim*) is over, Jews who have been uprooted from their homes can find lodging in the Holy Land. Let us not view this matter lightly! It is the voice of my Beloved that knocketh!

THE OBLIGATION OF TORAH JEWRY TO THE LAND OF ISRAEL

What was our reaction to the voice of the Beloved that knocketh, to God's bounteous kindnesses and wonders? Did we descend from our couches and immediately open the door? Or did we, like the Shulammite maiden, continue to rest and tarry rather than descend from our beds? "I have put off my coat; how shall I put it on? I have washed my feet; how shall I soil them?" (Song of Songs 5:3).

All of the trepidation and concern for the geographical integrity of the State of Israel, on the one hand, and all of our enemies' proposals that are designed to exact territorial concessions from the State of Israel, all of the brazen demands of the Arabs for boundary changes, on the other hand, are

all based on one and only one fact: the Jews have
not colonized the Negev and have not set up hundreds of settlements there. Were the Negev settled
by tens of thousands of Jews, then not even Nasser
would dream of the possibility of wresting it from
the State of Israel. Desolation, from time immemorial, endangers political tranquility. The Torah has
already emphasized this truth. "Thou mayest not
consume them [the nations of Canaan] quickly, lest
the beasts of the field increase upon thee"
(Deuteronomy 7:22). The fact that Jews conquered
the Negev does not suffice; the main thing is to set-
tle it. Maimonides, the great eagle, ruled that the
first sanctification of the land, wrought by Joshua,
was not permanent because it derived from military conquest, which was nullified by the invasion
of the enemy, whose army was mighty and
weapons many, who conquered the land and
seized it from us. The second sanctification,
wrought by Ezra, which derived from taking possession of the land and settling it—in accordance
with the divine command—with the toil of one's
hands and the sweat of one's brow, was not nullified.[8] The holiness grounded in settling the land—
settling, plain and simple—remains in effect for its
time and for eternity! We have been remiss and our
guilt is great. American Jewry could certainly have
accelerated the process of colonization. But why
should we search out the faults of others and seek
to place the blame on the shoulders of secular
Jews? Let us examine our own flaws and confess
our own sins. It is precisely Orthodox Jews, more
than all other American Jews, who bear the burden
of guilt for the slow place of conquest through tak-

ing possession. The obligation to pay close attention to the "voice of my Beloved" that knocketh
and to respond to Him immediately with mighty
deeds and undertakings devolves precisely upon
us who are faithful to traditional Judaism. Rashi,
basing himself upon the Sifra, in his commentary
on the verse "And I will bring the land into desolation" (Leviticus 26:32) states: "This is a good dis-
pensation for the Israelites, for the enemies will not
find any gratification in their land, since it will be
desolate of its inhabitants." The land of Israel cannot be built by just any people or group. Only the
Jewish people possesses the capacity to transform
it into a settled land and to make the desolate waste
bloom. This divine promise became a miraculous
fact in the history of the land of Israel during various periods. We must not forget, even for a
moment, that the land of Israel drew the nations of
the world—Christian and Muslim alike—to it like a
magnet. The medieval Crusades were undertaken
for the purpose of conquering the land of Israel and
colonizing it with a Christian population. All of the
efforts of the crusaders were in vain, and they did
not take root in the land. Even the Muslims, who
were already in the land, did not succeed in colonizing it properly. It remained a desolate waste.
"And your land shall be a desolation" (Leviticus
26:33). Even later, in the modern era, when the
European nations in the seventeenth and eigh-
teenth centuries settled and colonized entire conti-
nents, the land of Israel remained desolate and in a
more primitive state than its neighboring Arab
countries—Egypt, Syria, and Lebanon. Had the
land of Israel been settled by a capable, enterpris-

ing, powerful, and cultured nation, had it been
properly colonized and developed, then our tie to
it would, in the course of events, have been obliter-
ated, and no Jewish presence would have established itself there. Strangers would have consumed
its goodness and its fruit, and our rights and claims
would have been completely nullified. However,
the land of Israel did not betray the people of Israel;
she remained faithful to them and during all those
years awaited her redeemer. It stands to reason,
then, that when the possibility arose for the Jewish
people to return to its land, the land which had
withheld its treasures from strangers and guarded
them for us, Orthodox Jews would eagerly bestir
themselves to perform this great and important
commandment and would plunge, with joy and
enthusiasm, into the midst of this holy task—the
building and settling of the land. Alas, we did not
act thus. When the "desolate wife," who had awaited us with such yearning and for so long, invited
us, her sons, to come and redeem her from her desolate condition, and when the Beloved, Who had
watched over the desolation for almost nineteen
hundred years, and Who had decreed that not a
tree would flourish there, that no springs would
fructify its ground, knocked on the doors of His
love, the maiden—we religious Jews—did not rush
to descend from her couch and let in her Beloved.
Had we built a dense network of settlements
throughout the entire length of the land, from Eilat
to Dan, then our situation would be entirely different.

Let us be honest and speak openly and candidly.
We are critical of certain well-known Israeli leaders

because of their attitudes to traditional values and religious observances. Our complaints are valid; we have serious accusations to level against the secular leaders of the land of Israel. However, are they alone guilty, while we are as clean and pure as the ministering angels? Such an assumption is completely groundless! We could have extended our influence in shaping the spiritual image of the *Yishuv* if we had hastened to arouse ourselves from our sleep and descend to open the door for the Beloved Who was knocking. I am afraid that we Orthodox Jews are, even today, still sunk in a very pleasant slumber. Had we established more religious kibbutzim, had we built more houses for religious immigrants, had we created an elaborate and extended system of schools, our situation would be entirely other than it is. Then we would not have to criticize the leaders of other movements so severely. We Orthodox Jews suffer from a unique illness which is not to be found among nonreligious Jews (with a few exceptions); we are all misers! In comparison with other American Jews, we do not excel in the attribute of *ḥesed*. We are content to give a few pennies, and in return for our paltry contributions we demand a hefty this-worldly reward and a place at the head of the line. Therefore, our honor has declined to a new low, and we are not able to exercise the proper influence on Jewish life here and on events in the land of Israel. America, the great and the free, is a land of tzedakah, of charity. The American government itself, during the years 1945 to 1956, disbursed over $55 billion in foreign aid. (The numbers are simply unimaginable.) And it is only philanthropists, who know how to give, who are accorded honor in a land which knows how to give and help on such a scale. Consequently, we Orthodox Jews in America are not entitled to any position of eminence, and such positions are occupied by others. Recently, we have become specialists in criticism and in the detection of plagues—"and the priest shall look on the plague . . . and pronounce him unclean" (Leviticus 13:3). This task—to search out blemishes and offer our expert opinions—we know how to do very well. However, we have overlooked one point, namely, that the priest who declares a person unclean must go outside the camp to the leper, the afflicted individual, the sufferer, in order to purify him. "And the priest shall go outside the camp . . . and the priest shall command . . ." (Leviticus 14:3–4). We have to build not just small, isolated corners whose influence is not discernible but major institutions throughout the length and breadth of America and Israel. It is incumbent upon us to purify those who are "outside the camp," those who dwell in the great camp of ignorance. For this end we require great sums; and we Orthodox Jews are very far from being generous and liberal, open-hearted and open-handed, in matters of charity. This is why our institutions, both here and in the land of Israel, are so poverty-stricken. In particular, the religious *shivat ẓiyyon* (return to Zion) movement must, perforce, be content with meager sums. Because it is deprived of adequate financial means, it lacks the capacity to operate on a proper scale. Indeed, it is true: the faithful maiden is very lovely, her eyes are like doves, her face shines with grace and charm. She is much more beautiful than the nonreligious maiden. But "grace is deceitful and beauty is vain" (Proverbs 31:30) if the faithful maiden is miserly and slothful. "I have put off my coat; how shall I put it on? I have washed my feet; how shall I soil them?" (Song of Songs 5:3). If one telephones a rich Jew and asks that he contribute to a worthy cause, he replies: "I am going to Florida, and this year have decided to stay in a luxury hotel. I am, therefore, unable to give the amount requested of me." What did the rabbi say to the King of the Khazars? "This is a justified reproach, O King of the Khazars! . . . and that which we say, 'Bow to His holy hill' (Psalms 99:9), . . . is but as the chattering of the starling and the nightingale."[9]

Can we not hear, in our own concern for the peace and security of the land of Israel today, the knocking of the Beloved pleading with His love that she let Him enter? He has already been knocking for more than eight years and still has not received a proper response; nevertheless, He continues to knock. We have been fortunate. The Beloved did not show any special regard to His own cherished darling, but He continues to favor us. On that fateful night, the maiden's Beloved knocked on the door of her tent for only a brief moment and then disappeared, while He treats us with extreme patience. It is eight years now that He has been knocking. Would that we not miss the moment!

THE COVENANT AT SINAI
AND THE COVENANT IN EGYPT

When we probe the nature of our historical existence we arrive at a very important insight, one
that constitutes a fundamental element of our
worldview. The Torah relates that God made two
covenants with the Israelites. The first covenant He
made in Egypt: "And I will take you to Me for a
people, and I will be to you a God" (Exodus 6:7);
the second covenant, at Mount Sinai: "And he took
the book of the covenant . . . and said: 'Behold the
blood of the covenant, which the Lord hath made
with you in agreement with all these words'"
(Exodus 24:7–8). (The third covenant, "These are
the words of the covenant . . . beside the covenant
which He made with them in Horeb"
[Deuteronomy 28:69], is identical in content and
goals with the covenant at Sinai.)[10] What is the
nature of these two covenants? It seems to me that
this question is implicitly answered at the beginning of our essay. For just as Judaism distinguishes
between fate and destiny in the personal-individ-
ual realm, so it differentiates between these two
ideas in the sphere of our national historical existence. The individual is tied to his people both with
the chains of fate and with the bonds of destiny. In
the light of this premise, it may be stated that the
covenant in Egypt was a covenant of fate, while the
covenant at Sinai was a covenant of destiny.

THE COVENANT OF FATE

What is the nature of a covenant of fate? Fate in the life of a people, as in the life of an individual, signifies an existence of compulsion. A strange necessity binds the particulars into one whole. The individual, against his will, is subjected and subjugated to the national, fate-laden, reality. He cannot evade this reality and become assimilated into some other, different reality. The environment spits out the Jew who flees from the presence of the Lord, and he is bestirred from his slumber in the same manner as the prophet Jonah, who awoke upon hearing the voice of the ship's captain demanding that he identify himself in both personal and national-religious terms.

This sense of a fate-laden existence of necessity gives rise to the historical loneliness of the Jew. He is alone both in life and in death. The concept of a Jewish burial-plot emphasizes the Jew's strange isolation from the world. Let the sociologists and psychologists say what they may about the incomprehensible alienation of the Jew. All their explanations are naught but vain and empty speculations which do not shed any intelligible light on this phenomenon. Jewish loneliness belongs to, is part of, the framework of the covenant of fate that was made in Egypt. In truth, Judaism and separation from the world are identical ideas. Even before the exile in Egypt, with the appearance of the first Jew—our father, Abraham—loneliness entered our world. Abraham was lonely. He was called Abraham the Hebrew, *Avraham ha-'Ivri*, for "all the world was to one side ('*ever eḥad*), while he was to the other side (*'ever eḥad*)."[11] When Balaam saw the Jewish people dwelling tribe by tribe, he apprehended the mystery of the solitary mode of Jewish existence and proclaimed in a state of amazement: "Lo, it is a people that shall dwell alone, and shall not be reckoned among the nations" (Numbers 23:9). Even if a person achieves the pinnacle of social or political success, he will still not be able to free himself from the chains of isolation. This paradoxical fate has preserved both the separateness and the uniqueness of the Jew despite his supposed integration into his foreign, non-Jewish environment. Even as politically powerful a person as Joseph, who ranked next to the king of Egypt, lived separately from Egyptian society and dwelled alone in his tent—"And they set on for him by himself . . . and for the Egyptians that did eat with him, by themselves" (Genesis 43:32). Before his death, he pleaded with his brothers: "God will surely remember you, and ye shall carry up my bones from hence" (Genesis 50:25). Despite my greatness and glory, I am bound up with you and with your survival, both in my life and in my death. This special, incomprehensible reality of the individual clinging to the community and feeling alienated from the foreign, outside world became crystallized in Egypt. It was there that the Israelites raised themselves up to the rank of a people, peoplehood signifying both togetherness (the Hebrew word for "people," *'am*, is related to the Hebrew word *'im*, meaning "with," "togetherness")[12] and the uniqueness that derives from togetherness. This consciousness of a covenant of fate in all of its mani-

festations is an integral part of our historical-meta-
physical being.

When the Jew, with this sense of his special,
unique fate, confronts God face to face, he encoun-
ters the God of the Hebrews, Who reveals Himself
to man from out of the very midst of the experience
of loneliness and necessity, from out of the very
midst of the consciousness of the fate which seizes
hold of an individual and overcomes him. The God
of the Hebrews does not wait for man to search for
Him, to freely invite Him into his presence. He
imposes His rule over man against his will. A Jew
cannot expel the God of the Hebrews from his private domain. Even if he violates the Sabbath,
defiles his table and bed, and strives to deny his
own Jewishness, his membership in the Jewish
people, he will still not be able to escape the domin-
ion of the God of the Hebrews, Who pursues him
like a shadow. So long as a person's nose testifies to
his origins, so long as a drop of Jewish blood cours-
es through his veins, so long as physically he is still
a Jew, he serves the God of the Hebrews against his
will. Neither counsel nor understanding can pre-
vail against Him. Yea, if the Jew who rejects his
people ascends heavenward, yea, if he takes the
wings of the morning, there would the hand of the
God of the Hebrews take hold of him. Whither
shall the Jew go from the spirit of the God of the
Hebrews, and whither shall he flee from His presence? "And they said: 'The God of the Hebrews
hath met with us. Let us go, we pray thee, three
days' journey into the wilderness, and sacrifice
unto the Lord our God; lest He fall upon us with

pestilence, or with the sword'" (Exodus 5:3). To disregard the commands of the God of the Hebrews will, in the end, result in calamity and destruction.

The covenant of fate expresses itself as well in positive categories which derive from the consciousness of a shared fate. There are four aspects to this rare mode of consciousness.

First, the consciousness of a shared fate manifests itself as a consciousness of shared circumstances. We all find ourselves in the realm of a common fate which binds together all of the people's different strata, its various units and groups, a fate which does not discriminate between one group and another group or between one person and his fellow. Our fate does not distinguish between aristocrats and common folk, between rich and poor, between a prince garbed in the royal purple and a pauper begging from door to door, between a pietist and an assimilationist. Even though we speak a plethora of languages, even though we are inhabitants of different lands, even though we look different—one may be short and dark, the other tall and blond—, even though we live in varying and unequal social and economic conditions—one may dwell in a magnificent palace, the other in a miserable hovel—, we still share the same fate. If the Jew in the hovel is beaten, then the security of the Jew in the palace is endangered. "Think not with thyself that thou shalt escape in the king's house, more than all the Jews" (Esther 4:13). Both Queen Esther, garbed in royal apparel, and Mordecai the Jew, clad in sackcloth, were caught in the same web of historical circumstances. *Haverim kol Yisrael,* "All Israel are knit together"—We will all be pursued unto death or we will all be redeemed with an eternal salvation. Second, the consciousness of shared historical circumstances results in the experience of shared suffering. The feeling of sympathy is a fundamental feature of the consciousness of the unifying fate of the Jewish people. The suffering of one part of the people affects the people as a whole. The scattered and dispersed people mourn together and are comforted together. *Tefillah,* prayer, *ze'akah,* the human outcry, and *nehamah,* comfort, are all formulated, as I emphasized above, in the plural. The pleas that ascend from the abyss of affliction are not restricted to the suffering and pain of the individual supplicant. They include the needs of the entire community. When a person has a sick relative, he cannot pray for him alone, but has to pray for all the sick of Israel. If one enters into a mourner's home to comfort him and wipe away a tear from his grieving face, one directs one's words of comfort to all who mourn for Zion and Jerusalem. The slightest disturbance in the condition of a single individual or group ought to grieve all of the various segments of the people in all of their dispersions. It is both forbidden and impossible for the "I" to isolate himself from his fellow and not share in his suffering. If the premise of shared historical circumstances is correct, then the experience of shared suffering is the direct conclusion of that premise.

A preacher of the last generation put it well. He said that the Jewish people may be compared to the man with two heads, concerning whom the ques-

tion was posed in the house of study: How is he to
be viewed for purposes of inheritance? Does he
take two portions like a dual person? Or does he
take one portion like a single unified individual?[13]
One may similarly ask: Has the dispersion of the
Jewish people throughout the lands of its exile and
its taking root in its various surroundings resulted
in its spiritual and psychic dissolution? Or has the
unity of the people not been abrogated, despite the
fact that it has grown many heads, that it expresses
itself in a multitude of languages and cultures, in
differing customs and varying practices? In a
word: Is the Jewish diaspora a unity or not?

The answer—the preacher continued—to the
question of the unity of the Jewish people is identical with the ruling issued in the house of study
regarding the question of the unity of the two-
headed heir. Let boiling water be poured on one of
his heads, stated the judge, and let us see the reaction of the other head. If the other head cries out in
pain, then both heads blend into one complete and
unified personality, and the heir will take one portion. However, if the second head does not feel the
pangs of the first head, then we have two personal-
ities coupled together in one body, and they take
two portions.

The same holds true with regard to the question
of the unity of the Jewish people. The authoritative
ruling is that as long as there is shared suffering, in
the manner of "I will be with him in trouble"
(Psalms 91:15), there is unity. If the Jew upon
whom divine providence has shed a beneficent
light, and who consequently believes that, at least
with respect to him, the venom of hate and rejec-

tion has been expunged from his surroundings, still feels the troubles of the people and the burden of a fate-laden existence, then his link with the people has not been broken. If boiling water is poured upon the head of the Jew in Morocco, the fashionably attired Jew in Paris or London has to scream at the top of his voice, and through feeling the pain he will remain faithful to his people. The fragmentation of the people and the blearing of its image are concomitants of the absence of the feeling of sympathy.

Third, shared suffering finds its expression in the awareness of shared responsibility and liability. When Israel went forth from Egypt, Moses and Aaron fell down upon their faces, pleaded with God, and said: "O God, the God of the spirits of all flesh, shall one man sin, and will Thou be wroth with all the congregation?" (Numbers 16:22). This prayer accomplished the aim intended for it by Moses and Aaron, the shepherds of their people, Israel; God agreed that they had acted properly in setting forth their plea and punished only the congregation of Korah. However, God's display of this particular mode of *ḥesed* was only temporary. On a permanent basis, the "I" is held responsible for the sin of his fellow, if it was in his power to rebuke him, to protest against his behavior and induce him to repent. A collective ethico-halakhic responsibility devolves upon the entire Jewish people. The individuals coalesce into one ethico-halakhic unit, possessed of one conscience and an all-encompassing normative consciousness. The halakhah has already declared that all Jews are guarantors for one another. Consequently, the halakhic ruling is that a person who has already discharged his obligation to fulfill a commandment can still perform the commandment for his fellow Jew who has not as yet performed it and thereby enable him to discharge his obligation. The fact that the first person has already performed the commandment does not result in his being included in the category of those who are exempt from a particular obligation, who cannot enable the many to discharge their obligation. The "I" is not himself exempt as long as his fellow has not performed the commandment required of him. A special covenant was made in order to effect the mutual *'arevut* (suretyship) of all Jews for one another. This covenant received its expression in the blessings and curses on Mounts Gerizim and Ebal. It is based on the idea of peoplehood that God revealed to Moses in Egypt. From the idea of peoplehood the covenant of mutual *'arevut* directly followed. Moses, the master of the prophets, in referring to this covenant of *'arevut*, emphatically proclaimed: "that He may establish thee this day unto Himself for a people and that He may be unto thee a God" (Deuteronomy 29:12). In speaking thus, he used the same phrases employed to describe the covenant in Egypt, "And I will take you to Me for a people, and I will be to you a God" (Exodus 6:7). Here the concept of shared fate has risen from the plane of socio-political suffering to the plane of ethico-halakhic *'arevut*. We are all mutually responsible for one another, we are all each other's guarantors, as the verse states: "but the things that are revealed belong unto us and our children for ever, that we may do all the words of this Law" (Deuteronomy 29:28).[14]

Shared responsibility is not only a theoretical halakhic idea; it is also a central fact in the history of the Jewish people in respect to its relationship to the nations of the world. Our neighbors have always condemned all of us for the sins of one of us; they have, thereby, transformed the rhetorical talmudic query, "Shall Tuviah sin and Zigud be punished?" (Pesaḥim 113b), into a daily reality that does not even surprise anyone. The identification of the actions of the individual with the deeds of the people is a fundamental feature of our history. Our enemies will not allow the individual Jew to remain isolated in his own private, separate sphere. They take him out of his four cubits into the public domain, and there they make use of him in order to level a harsh indictment against the entire community. This criterion they apply only to Jews and not to other nations. No one has ever accused a particular Russian or Chinese of being an agent of international communism simply because racially he belongs to a people who have instituted a communist regime in their own country and seek to forcibly impose their cruel reign on the entire world. In contrast to this logical and humane approach which is applied to other peoples, the Jewish people, as a whole, on account of the deeds of a few Jewish apostates, is libeled as being an adherent of communism. We have still not been cleared of this libel. Again, the various explanations of this phenomenon offered by scholars are unsatisfying. It makes no difference if the root of the problem is assigned to the psychic-conative sphere or the political-historical sphere. Such scientific classification is of no value; the phenomenon remains opaque and mysterious. For us, as religious Jews, there is only one answer to this enigma: It is the hand of the covenant of fate that was made in Egypt regarding the absolute uniqueness of the Jewish people which manifests itself through this otherwise incomprehensible reality.

The commandment of the sanctification of the divine Name and the prohibition against the desecration of the divine Name[15] can be explained very well in the light of this principle of shared responsibility and liability. The actions of the individual are charged to the account of the community. Any sin he commits besmirches the name of Israel in the world. The individual, therefore, must answer not only to his own personal conscience but also to the collective conscience of the people. If he behaves properly, he sanctifies the name of Israel and the Name of the God of Israel; if he sins, he casts shame and disgrace on the people and desecrates the Name of its God.

Fourth, shared historical circumstances give rise to shared activity. The obligation to give charity and perform deeds of lovingkindness derives its force from the all-penetrating and all-encompassing experience of brotherhood. The Torah, in laying down these commandments, uses the term *aḥ*, "brother," instead of *re'sa*, "fellow." "And if thy brother be waxen poor . . . then thou shalt uphold him . . . and he shall live with thee" (Leviticus 25:35). "Thou shalt not harden thy heart, nor shut thy hand from thy needy brother.... Thou shalt surely open thy hand unto thy poor and needy brother in thy land" (Deuteronomy 15:7, 11). The confrontation with the people's strange and unusual fate-laden existence endows the Jew with a unifying consciousness in the field of social action. The common situation of all Jews without distinction—whether manifested on the objective level as shared historical circumstances or on the subjective level as shared suffering—opens up founts of mercy and lovingkindness in the heart of the individual on behalf of his brethren in trouble, which indirectly affects him as well. Maimonides formulated this idea in his unique style, at once highly concise and overflowing with ideas:

> All Israelites and those who have attached themselves to them are to each other like brothers, as it is said, "Ye are the children of the Lord your God" (Deuteronomy 14:1). If brother shows no compassion to brother, who will show compassion to him? And unto whom shall the poor of Israel raise their eyes? Unto the heathens, who hate them and persecute them? Their eyes are therefore uplifted solely to their brethren.[16]

We have stated that it is the consciousness of the fate imposed upon the people against their will and of their terrible isolation that is the source of the people's unity, of their togetherness. It is precisely this consciousness as the source of the people's togetherness that gives rise to the attribute of *hesed*, which summons and stirs the community of fate to achieve a positive mode of togetherness through ongoing, joint participation in its own historical circumstances, in its suffering, conscience, and acts of mutual aid. The lonely Jew finds consolation in breaking down the existential barriers of egoism and alienation, joining himself to his fellow and actively connecting himself with the community. The oppressive sense of fate undergoes a positive transformation when individual personal existences blend together to form a new unit—a people. The obligation to love one another stems from the consciousness of this people of fate, this lonely people that inquires into the meaning of its own uniqueness. It is this obligation of love that stands at the very heart of the covenant made in Egypt.

COVENANT OF DESTINY

What is the nature of the covenant of destiny? Destiny in the life of a people, as in the life of an individual, signifies a deliberate and conscious existence that the people has chosen out of its own free will and in which it finds the full realization of its historical being. Its existence, in place of simply being the experience of an unalterable reality into which the people has been thrust, now appears as the experience of an act possessing teleological dimensions, replete with movement, ascent, striving, and attaining. The people is embedded in its destiny as a result of its longing for a refined, substantive, and purposeful existence. Destiny is the flowing spring of the people's unique exaltation: It is the unceasing stream of supernal influence that will never dry up as long as the people charts its path in accordance with the divine Law. A life of destiny is a life with direction; it is the fruit of cognitive readiness and free choice.

The covenant in Egypt was made against the

Israelites' will. God took them unto Himself for a
people without consulting them beforehand, as the
verse states: "And I will take you to Me for a people" (Exodus 6:7). The covenant at Sinai, in contrast, was first presented to the Israelites before it
was made. God sent Moses to the Israelites to bring
them His word, and Moses returned to God with
their response. The halakhah views the covenant at
Sinai as a contract that can be drawn up only with
the knowledge and consent of the party assuming
obligations for the future, in this instance the community of Israel. The proclamation "We will do
and obey" (Exodus 24:7) constitutes the foundation
of the acceptance of the Torah.[17]

What is the content of the covenant at Sinai? It
consists in a special way of life which directs man's
existence toward attaining a single goal, a goal
beyond the reach of the man of fate, namely, man's
imitation of his Creator through an act of self-tran-
scendence. The creative activity which suffuses the
covenant of destiny flows from a source unknown
to the man of fate. It derives from man's rebellion
against a life of sheer facticity, from the desire pul-
sating within him for more exalted, more supernal
modes of being. The deeds of lovingkindness and
brotherhood which are interwoven into the
covenant at Sinai have as their motivating force not
the Jew's strange sense of isolation, but rather his
experience of the unity of a people forever
betrothed to the one true God. The absolute unity
of God is reflected in the unity of the people bound
to Him eternally. "Thou art One and Thy Name is
One, and who is like unto Thy people, Israel, one
nation on earth?" Jewish fellowship in this dimen-

sion is a result of the special filial relationship the members of this people enjoy with God. "We are Thy children and Thou art our Father." (Maimonides emphasized this motif in the passage we cited earlier.) At Sinai, God raised on high the covenant of fate which He made with a community which, against its will, finds itself alone, a community the members of which perform deeds of lovingkindness on behalf of one another as a result of this externally imposed isolation and separateness, and transformed the covenant of fate into a covenant of destiny which He made with a community possessing will and desire, a community sanctifying itself and directing itself toward encountering God. The "people," lacking direction and purpose (the Hebrew word for "people," *'am*, as we have already noted, is related to the word *'im*, "with"), became a "nation," which signifies a community possessing a distinct communal countenance and collective physiognomy (the Hebrew word for "nation" is *goy*, which is related to the word *geviyah*, "body").[18] The *'am-ḥesed*, the people of lovingkindness, was raised on high and became a *goy kadosh*, a holy nation.[19] Holiness, which expresses itself in the form of an authentic mode of being, is the very foundation of the shared destiny of the nation.[20]

When the man of destiny confronts God he beholds the God of Israel, who reveals Himself to man only with his consent and at his invitation. The God of Israel enters into a relationship with finite, creaturely man only after the latter has sanctified himself and purified himself from all uncleanliness and pollution, and awaits, with passion and longing, this wondrous encounter. The revelation of the God of Israel does not take place under all circumstances and conditions. Such a revelation demands a special spiritual state, as set forth in the divine command, "Be ready for the third day" (Exodus 19:11). Without such preparation, such readiness on the part of man, the God of Israel will not just randomly and casually reveal Himself. The God of Israel does not take man by surprise. Rather, He responds to man's fervid plea. However, the God of Israel takes no interest in the person who does not passionately yearn for Him with a longing that expresses itself in and takes the form of concrete actions. While the God of the Hebrews pursues man against his will and takes no heed of his opinions or wishes, the God of Israel consults with man prior to the encounter. Already in Egypt the Almighty revealed Himself to Moses not only as the God of the Hebrews but also as the God of Israel, Who awaits man and invites him to serve Him. "Thus saith the Lord, God of Israel: Let My people go, that they may hold a feast unto Me in the wilderness" (Exodus 5:1).

CAMP AND CONGREGATION

In order to explain the difference between the people of fate and the nation of destiny, it is worth taking note of another antithesis, namely, the antithesis between camp (*mahaneh*) and congregation (*'edah*). The Torah has used both terms together in speaking of the Israelites. "Make thee two trumpets of silver, of beaten work shalt thou make them; and they shall be unto thee for the calling of the congregation and for causing the camp to set forward" (Numbers 10:2).

Camp and congregation constitute two distinct sociological phenomena, two separate groups lacking any common features, devoid of any symbiotic relationship. The camp is created as a result of the desire for self-defense and is nurtured by a sense of fear; the congregation is created as a result of the longing for the realization of an exalted ethical idea and is nurtured by the sentiment of love. Fate reigns, in unbounded fashion, in the camp; destiny reigns in the congregation. The camp constitutes a particular stage in the historical development of the people, while the existence of the nation is identical with that of the congregation.

The camp, by its nature, does not constitute a distinctly human phenomenon. In the animal kingdom as well, we can already discern the glimmers of this phenomenon. There, too, the camp serves as protection against harm. Let flocks of sheep and cattle suddenly sense that danger is lurking somewhere, and, overcome by panic, they will confusedly stream down from every green mountain and high pasture and hastily herd together, interlock their horns, and press their heads one against the other. Fear finds its instinctive mechanical expression in the quest for survival through sheer physical contiguity. The primitive urge for individual mute creatures to come together in face of opposition and danger and form one camp is a basic feature of the animal instinct.

In the human realm as well, the camp is created only as a result of fear. When a person is terror-stricken by his involuntary fate-laden existence, he grasps his own helplessness and joins with his fellows both for protection from and victory over the enemy. The organization of a camp serves as a military tactic. Consider the phraseology used by the Torah: "When thou goest forth in camp against thine enemies" (Deuteronomy 23:10). The camp is born out of the dread of extinction and annihilation, out of the fear imposed upon it by fate. From the camp there emerges the people. The Israelites in Egypt were a camp to begin with; when God freed them they attained the rank of a people.

However, the congregation constitutes a distinctive human phenomenon; it is an expression of man's powerful spirit. The congregation is a typically human creation, a creation imbued with the splendor of the human personality. The congregation is created not as a result of negative factors, as a result of the fear of fate that pursues the man who senses his misery and weakness, but as a result of positive drives. The foundation of the congregation is destiny. A congregation is a group of individuals possessing a common past, a common future, common goals and desires, a common aspiration for a world which is wholly good and beautiful, and a common, unique, and unified destiny. The beginning of the congregation is grounded in the traditions of the Patriarchs, in the people's heritage, reaching back to its obscure dawn, while its end is rooted in a shared eschatological vision. The Hebrew word for "congregation," *'edah*, is related to the Hebrew word for "witness," *'ed*. The members of the congregation are witnesses.[21] And to what do they bear witness if not to events that are long since past, and to a wondrous future that has not yet arrived? The congregation encompasses not only the individuals living in the here-and-now but all who have lived and all who will live, from time immemorial until the eschaton. The dead, who have long since passed away, continue to abide in the realm of the congregation; and those who are yet to be born are already living in its domain. The congregation is a holy nation that has no fear of fate and is not compelled to live against its will. It believes in its own destiny, and it dedicates itself, out of its own free will, to the realization of that destiny. The covenant in Egypt was made with a people born from a camp; the covenant at Sinai was made with a holy nation.

CONVERSION THROUGH CIRCUMCISION AND IMMERSION

The individual's participation in the fate and the destiny of the chosen people-nation, and his experience of belonging to Keneset Israel, the Jewish community, as a complete entity which actualizes, through its historical existence, the two ideas of *ḥesed*, lovingkindness, and *kedushah*, holiness, together—such participation and such an experience of belonging are indissoluble and indivisible. The covenant at Sinai consummated the covenant in Egypt. Destiny attached itself to fate; both became one distinct covenantal unit. It is impossible to formulate a worldview that opposes the unity of the people of lovingkindness and the holy nation; that which belongs together cannot be sundered. A Jew who participates in his people's suffering and fate but does not bind himself to its destiny, which expresses itself in a life of Torah and mitzvot, violates a fundamental principle of Judaism and impairs his own singularity. Conversely, a Jew who does not grieve over the afflictions of his people, but seeks to separate himself from the Jewish fate, desecrates the holiness of Israel, even if he observes the commandments.[22]

Therefore, a Gentile who comes to attach himself to the Jewish community must accept upon himself the yoke of both covenants. He must enter into the magic circle of Jewish fate and, in a spirit of holiness, dedicate himself to Jewish destiny. Conversion consists in a person's joining himself to both the people formed by the covenant in Egypt and the holy nation formed by the covenant at Sinai. Take heed of a fundamental principle: There can be no partial conversion, and one cannot relinquish even the slightest iota of either of the two covenants. The devotion to Keneset Israel, both as a people whom God, with a strong hand, took unto Himself in Egypt, a people with its own history, suffering, sense of mutual responsibility, and commitment to deeds of mutual aid, and as a holy nation, committed, heart and soul, to the God of Israel and to His ethico-halakhic demands—this dual yet unified devotion is the most basic foundation of Judaism and the most fundamental feature of undergoing conversion.

Therefore, the halakhah has ruled that a convert who is circumcised but does not immerse himself, or immerses himself but is not circumcised, is not a proper convert until he is both circumcised and immerses himself. The act of circumcision (*milah*) was the charge given to Abraham the Hebrew, *Avraham ha-'Ivri*, the father of Jewish fate; it was performed by the Israelites in Egypt prior to their sacrificing and eating the paschal lamb, the symbol of the redemption from Egypt. For this reason it signifies the people's special fate, its isolation and its involuntary singularity. Circumcision is the *ot*, the sign incised in the very physical being of the Jew. It is a permanent sign between the God of the Hebrews and His people, a sign that cannot be effaced. If the flesh does not have the covenant of fate impressed upon it, then the singularity of the people is missing and the Gentile remains outside the bounds of the covenant in Egypt.

The act of immersion (*tevilah*), in contrast to that of circumcision, denotes the integration of a person in a great destiny and his entry into the covenant at Sinai. The Jews were charged with the commandment of immersion prior to the revelation of the Law at Sinai.[23] Immersion signifies purification and ascension from the profane to the sacred, from an ordinary, prosaic life to a life replete with an exalted vision. When the convert arises from his immersion, a spiritual reality suffused with destiny is newly formed within him, and he becomes sanctified with the holiness of Israel. It is not for naught that the act of acceptance of the yoke of the commandments is linked with the act of immersion.[24] For immersion, at its core, has as its sole purpose the representation of the experience of the revelation of the Law and of the ascension of a people, through a freely assumed obligation to perform the divine command, to the rank of a holy nation. If a

Gentile was circumcised but did not immerse himself, he lacks that personal bond to Jewish destiny. Such a Gentile has disassociated himself from the covenant at Sinai and from an ethico-halakhic identification with the holy nation. In the conversion formula to be found in the Book of Ruth, both these aspects are set forth, and their gist is succinctly expressed in its last two phrases: "Thy people shall be my people, and thy God, my God" (Ruth 1:16).

MELANCHOLY REFLECTIONS AND CONFESSIONS

Let us ask a simple question: Have we not sinned against the covenant of fate, the covenant made with a camp-people? Have we not transgressed against our obligation to participate in the suffering of the people, to witness and feel its burdens, as the verse states, "and he [Moses] witnessed their burdens" (Exodus 2:11, and cf. Rashi ad loc.)? Let us be frank: During the terrible Holocaust, when European Jewry was being systematically exterminated in the ovens and crematoria, the American Jewish community did not rise to the challenge, did not act as Jews possessing a properly developed consciousness of our shared fate and shared suffering, as well as the obligation of shared action that follows therefrom, ought to have acted. We did not sufficiently empathize with the anguish of the people and did very little to save our afflicted brethren. It is hard to know how much we might have accomplished had we tried harder. Personally, I think that we might have been able to save many. There is no doubt, however, that had we properly grieved over the afflictions of our brothers, had we raised our voices and forcefully demanded that Roosevelt issue a sharp protest-warning, backed by concrete actions, we could have substantially slowed the process of mass murder. We were witnesses to the greatest and most terrible tragedy in our history and we were silent. I do not wish to enter here into a discussion of details. This is a very sad and disturbing chapter in our history. But we all sinned by our silence in the face of the murder of millions. Have we not been summoned before the divine judgment seat to answer for our terrible transgression against the prohibition "Thou shalt not stand idly by the blood of thy fellow" (Leviticus 19:16), particularly when we stood idly by not just the blood of our *fellow* but the blood of our *fellows*, in their millions! And when I say "we," I mean all of us—myself included—rabbis and laymen, Orthodox and free-thinkers, the entire spectrum of Jewish political organizations: "your heads, your tribes, your elders, and your officers, even all the men of Israel . . . from the hewer of thy wood unto the drawer of thy water" (Deuteronomy 29:9–10). Do you know why we were so indifferent? Because our sense of peoplehood was flawed. We did not properly grasp the whole concept of shared fate and what it means to be a people. We lacked, as did Job to begin with, the attribute of *ḥesed*. It was because Job did not possess the sense of shared historical circumstances and shared suffering that he did not know how to pray on behalf of his friends. He was concerned only for his own well-being and for that of his family. In us, as well, the experience of a camp-people was absent. Therefore, we failed to offer up prayers on behalf of our brothers, both prayers of the heart and prayers consisting of vigorous deeds of rescue. Divine providence is testing us once again via the crisis that has overtaken the land of Israel. Let it be clearly stated: The matter does not just affect the political future of the land of Israel. The designs of the Arabs are directed not just against the political sovereignty of the State of Israel but against the very existence of the *Yishuv* in the land of Israel. They wish to destroy, heaven forbid, the entire community, "both men and women, infant and suckling, ox and sheep" (1 Samuel 15:3). At a Mizrachi convention I cited the view expressed by my father and master [R. Moses Soloveitchik] of blessed memory, that the proclamation, "The Lord will have war with Amalek from generation to generation" (Exodus 17:16) does not only translate into the communal exercise of waging obligatory war against a specific race but includes as well the obligation to rise up as a community against any people or group that, filled with maniacal hatred, directs its enmity against Keneset Israel. When a people emblazons on its banner, "Come, and let us cut them off from being a nation; that the name of Israel may be no more in remembrance" (Psalms 83:5) it becomes, thereby, Amalek.[25] In the 1930s and 1940s the Nazis, with Hitler at their head, filled this role. They were the Amalekites, the standard-bearers of insane hatred and enmity during the era just past. Today their place has been taken over by the mobs of Nasser and the Mufti. If we are silent now as well, I know not the verdict that will be issued against us by the God of justice. Do not rely on the "liberal" world's sense of equity. Those same righteous liberals were around fifteen years ago, and they looked with indifference upon the extermination of millions of people; they did not even lift a finger. If, heaven forbid, yet a second spectacle of blood were to take place before their very eyes, it is likely that they would not even lose a night's sleep over it.

Let us, like Job, learn to pray on behalf of our friends. Let us feel the pain of the *Yishuv*. We must understand *that the fate of the* Yishuv *in the land of Israel is our fate as well.* The Arabs have declared war not only against the State of Israel but against all of Keneset Israel. They now are the leaders of the international anti-Semitic movement and are among its main financial supporters, lavishing vast sums upon it. Let us overcome that foolish and unworthy fear of "dual loyalty" that our enemies have managed to infect us with. First, we will never be able to acquit ourselves in the eyes of anti-Semites, and whatever we do will not satisfy them. Second, as was stated above, this is not just a matter of ensuring the existence of the State but involves coming to the rescue, the physical rescue, of masses of Jews. Is it not our sacred obligation to come to their aid? Are we to be forbidden to demand that the *Yishuv* be properly defended? We find ourselves confronted with the very same type of test that confronted Job—the need to offer prayer on behalf of one's friends, prayer comprised of deeds and self-sacrifice. And in our case, *our* friends are the entire *Yishuv* in the land of Israel.

We have to do but one thing—open the door to the Beloved Who is knocking—and immediately all the dangers will cease.

THE VISION OF THE RELIGIOUS "SHIVAT ẒIYYON" MOVEMENT: ISOLATION AND SOLITUDE

What attitude ought the religious *shivat ẓiyyon* movement adopt vis-à-vis secular Zionism? It seems to me that political, nonreligious Zionism has committed one grave and fundamental error, an error based upon a false premise that secular Zionism introduced into the concept of the covenant in Egypt, the covenant of fate. With the establishment of the State of Israel, secular Zionism declares, we have become a people like all peoples, and the notion of "a people that dwells alone" (Numbers 23:29) has lost its validity. The extremists in the movement even wish to undermine the idea of one common fate—the fate of the camp-people—shared by the Jews in the diaspora and the Jews in the land of Israel. This entire line of thought is not just a philosophical-historical error but also a practical mistake. Under the influence of this spirit of indiscriminate amity, this doctrine of the sameness of all peoples, the representatives of the State of Israel have oftentimes displayed an embarrassing naivete, improperly evaluated particular circumstances and situations, and failed to discern the hidden intentions of certain individuals. As a result of their childlike innocence, they trust the promises of people who promptly proceed to betray us

and are overly impressed by flattery and blandish-
ments. It appears to me that on a number of occasions the foreign policy of the State of Israel has
manifested an absence of a sense of honor, of
national pride, of caution, and of the fortitude to
staunchly maintain one's own position.

All these mistakes flow from the initial error
committed by secular Zionism when it sought to
erase the sense of isolation and perhaps even the
phenomenon of shared suffering from the book of
our history. The voice of the Beloved knocking
ought to open the eyes of all of us, even the most
avowed secularists among us. The State of Israel
has not been able and will not be able to abrogate
the force of the covenant, "And I will take you to
Me for a people" (Exodus 6:7), and to liquidate the
shared fate that is the source of Jewish isolation.
The State of Israel today is isolated in precisely the
same manner that the Jewish people has been isolated during the thousands of years of its history. If
anything, the isolation of the State today is even
more striking than the isolation of the Jewish people in the past, for the present-day isolation manifests itself in the international arena. "They hold
crafty converse against Thy people, and take counsel against Thy treasured ones. They have said:
'Come and let us cut them off from being a nation;
that the name of Israel may be no more in remembrance.' For they have consulted together with one
consent; against Thee do they make a covenant; the
tents of Edom and the Ishmaelites; Moab and the
Hagrites; Gebol and Ammon and Amalek; Philistia
with the inhabitants of Tyre; Assyria is also joined
with them. They have been an arm to the children

of Lot. Selah" (Psalms 83:4–9). Communist Russia together with the Catholic Vatican; Nehru, the disciple of Gandhi, together with the devout Catholic, Franco; the British Foreign Office together with Chiang Kai Shek—all have banded together in the attempt to isolate the State of Israel, and they are assisted in their attempt by our enemies in other lands. This conspiracy has taken place after the establishment of the State, during a time when many of its leaders thought that the State had solved the Jewish problem, that it had brought Jewish isolation to an end and had introduced normalcy into our existence. The premise that the State has weakened anti-Semitism is simply wrong. On the contrary, anti-Semitism has grown in strength and now, as part of its war against us, makes use of false libels against the State of Israel. Who can foresee the outcome of this anti-Semitic hatred? The validity of the covenant in Egypt cannot be abrogated by human hands. We continue to be a nation, scattered and dispersed, but, at the same time, bound up with one another. *Our fate is the fate of the Yishuv, and vice versa: The fate of the Yishuv is our fate.* Let no part of the Jewish people delude itself into vainly seeking "to escape in the king's house, more than all the Jews" (Esther 4:13). Each and every one of us is obliged to pray on behalf of his fellow. The Jews of America are forbidden to be quiet or to relax as long as the danger confronting the State of Israel persists. Nor can the inhabitants of the Holy Land prattle on about such nonsense as "the new type of Jew" being created there who has nothing in common with the diaspora Jew. All of us are obliged to attend to "the voice of my Beloved that knocketh."

However, the error of secular Zionism is more
serious than its simply not understanding the true
meaning of the covenant in Egypt, the covenant of
a camp-people, which takes the form of shared fate
and involuntary isolation. Secular Zionism has
sinned as well against the covenant at Sinai, the
covenant made with a holy congregation-nation,
which finds its expression in the shared destiny of
a sanctified existence. Only the religious *shivat
ziyyon* movement, with its traditional and authentic approach, has the capacity to rectify these dis-
tortions. If you were to ask me: What is the task of
the State of Israel? I would answer: The mission of
the State of Israel is neither the termination of the
unique isolation of the Jewish people nor the abrogation of its unique fate—in this it will not succeed!—but the elevation of a camp-people to the
rank of a holy congregation-nation and the transformation of shared fate to shared destiny. We
must remember, as was emphasized earlier, that
fate expresses itself primarily in an existence of
necessity, in the inability to escape from Judaism,
in the compulsion to suffer as a Jew. However, this
is not the Torah's goal, nor is it the ideal set forth
by our worldview. Our sense of unity with Keneset
Israel, according to the authentic view of Judaism,
must remain incomplete as long as it derives from
the covenant of fate made with a camp-people living an existence of compulsion, a covenant to
which we are bound by external constraints; it can
be complete only if it derives from the covenant
made with a holy congregation-nation, from the
covenant of shared destiny. An existence of fate
cannot satisfy man. On the contrary, it only inflicts

pain upon him. The sense of isolation is highly destructive. It can crush man, both body and spirit, can paralyze his faculties, can stop up the flowing wellspring of personal creativity. In particular, this sense weighs heavily on man because isolation per se lacks meaning and purpose. The lonely, isolated sufferer wonders: Wherefore and why? This isolation, which pursues man like a shadow, dulls his powers, his sense of awareness. Not so is the existence of destiny based upon the covenant made at Mount Sinai! Through this covenant, the "people"—a concept signifying subjection to the decree of an existence of necessity, participation in blind suffering, and the sensation of meaningless isolation—becomes transformed into a "holy nation" and attains the exalted rank of an ethico-religious congregation. From the depths of the consciousness of destiny a person can draw vigor and strength, creative powers, and the bliss of a renewed, free, and vibrant existence.

Let us review yet once again what was stated earlier. How do fate and destiny differ? In two ways. First, fate entails an existence of necessity; destiny is a freely willed existence, created by man himself as he chooses and charts his own path in life. Second, fate expresses itself in a bare, teleologically blank existence; destiny possesses both significance and purpose. A shared fate is simply the inability to rebel against fate; it is the tragic, Jonah-like incapacity to flee from before the God of the Hebrews. "But the Lord hurled a great wind into the sea so that the ship was like to be broken" (Jonah 1:4). A shared destiny means the unconstrained ability of the will to strive toward a goal; it means the free decision to devote oneself to an ideal; it means yearning for God. Jonah, in the end, cast off the blind fate pursuing him and chose the exalted destiny of the God of Israel. "I am a Hebrew and I fear the Lord, the God of heaven" (Jonah 1:9).

To be sure, there is an element of separation present even in the experience of a shared destiny; however, the separation entailed by destiny differs completely from that entailed by fate. It is not the negative feeling described in the prophetic vision of Balaam, "Lo, it is a people that shall dwell alone" (Numbers 23:9), but rather a unique consciousness vouchsafed by Moses, in the last hours before his death, to Keneset Israel, "And Israel dwelleth in security, alone the fountain of Jacob" (Deuteronomy 33:28). In truth, this separation is naught but the solitude of a pure and holy, splendid and glorious existence. It is the solitude that finds its expression in a person's uniqueness, in his divine image, and in his existential "I" experience. It is the solitude of the soul that dwells in concealment, in the depths of being; it is the solitude that is to be identified with a person's spirituality and individuality; it is the solitude that makes manifest man's dignity and freedom; it is the solitude of Moses, whose great spirit and exalted vision were beyond the people's comprehension; it is the solitude of Elijah and the rest of the prophets; it is the solitude concerning which Abraham spoke when he told his young men, "Abide ye here with the ass, and I and the lad will go yonder; and we will worship" (Genesis 22:5). While isolation involves harmful inferiority feelings deriving from self-negation, a person's solitude testifies to both his greatness and his sanctity, the greatness that is contained within his private domain and the sanctity that permeates the inner recesses of his unique consciousness. Loneliness robs man of his tranquility; solitude bestows upon him security, worth, and dignity—"security, alone."

Judaism has always believed, as we emphasized at the beginning of our remarks, that a person has the ability to take his fate in his hands and to mold it into destiny, into a life of freedom, meaning, and joy, that he has the power to transform isolation into solitude, a sense of inferiority into a feeling of worth. It is for this reason that Judaism has emphasized the importance of the principle of free will; it is for this reason that it has attached such great value to human reason, which enables man to liberate himself from subjugation to nature and rule over his environment and subject it to his will. The Jewish community is obliged to utilize its free will in all areas of life in general, but in particular on behalf of the welfare of the State of Israel. If secular Zionism should finally realize that the State of Israel cannot terminate the paradoxical fate of Jewish isolation—that, to the contrary, the incomprehensible isolation of "And I will take you to Me for a people" (Exodus 6:7) has become even more pronounced in the international arena—then it must put to itself the ancient query: "What is thine occupation? and whence comest thou? and of what people art thou?" (Jonah 1:8). This question will be asked of us one way or another. If we do not ask it of ourselves, then the non-Jew will put it to us; and we must answer proudly, "I fear the Lord, the God of Heaven" (Jonah 1:9). Our historic obligation, today, is to raise ourselves from a people to a holy nation, from the covenant of Egypt to the covenant at Sinai, from an existence of necessity to an authentic way of life suffused with eternal ethical and religious values, from a camp to a congregation. The task confronting the religious *shivat ziyyon* movement is to achieve that great union of the two covenants—Egypt and Sinai, fate and destiny, isolation and solitude. This task embraces utilizing our afflictions to improve ourselves, and spinning a web of *hesed* that will bind together all the parts of the people and blend them into one congregation, "one nation in the land"; it involves the readiness to pray for one's fellow, and empathy with his joy and grief. As the end result of this self-improvement we will achieve the holiness conferred by an existence of destiny and will ascend the mountain of the Lord. One great goal unites us all, one exalted vision sets all our hearts aflame. One Torah—the Written Torah and the Oral Torah—directs all of us toward one unified end: the realization of the vision of solitude, the vision of a camp-people that has ascended to the rank of a holy congregation-nation, bound together its fate with its destiny, and proclaims to the entire world, in the words of our ancient father, Abraham: "And I and the lad will go yonder, and we will worship and we will return to you" (Genesis 22:5).

—Translated from the Hebrew by
Lawrence Kaplan

Rabbi Soloveitchik's essay was originally delivered as an address at a public assembly on Yom ha-Aẓma'ut at Yeshivat Rabbenu Yitzḥak Elḥanan of Yeshiva University in New York City, 1956.

NOTES

1. See Berakhot 7a. According to R. Meir, Moses did not receive a reply to his request to comprehend the problem of suffering in the world—the righteous man who is in adversity and the wicked man who prospers. R. Yoḥanan in the name of R. Yose disagrees. Maimonides, in the *Guide of the Perplexed*, adopts the view of R. Yoḥanan in the name of R. Yose and asserts that God enlightened Moses regarding the governance of the totality of existence. See *Guide* 1:54: "This dictum—'All My goodness' (Exodus 33:19)—alludes to the display to him [Moses] of all existing things . . . that is, he has grasped the existence of all My world with a true and firmly established understanding."

2. The medieval authorities (*Rishonim*) already discussed the issue of a man being deprived of choice because of his being extremely steeped in sin. See Maimonides, Laws of Repentance 6:3; and Naḥmanides' *Commentary on the Torah* to Exodus 7:3, 9:12.

3. The connection between trouble and repentance finds its expression in the commandment to cry out and sound the alarm with trumpets whenever trouble befalls the community. Maimonides, in Laws of Fast Days 1:1–4, states: "It is a positive scriptural commandment to cry out and sound the alarm with trumpets whenever trouble befalls the community, as it is said, 'against the adversary that oppresseth you, then ye shall sound the alarm with the trumpets' (Numbers 10:9), that is to say: Whatever is oppressing you, whether it be

famine, pestilence, locusts, or the like, cry out over them and sound the trumpets. This procedure is one of the paths of repentance, for when trouble occurs and they cry out over it and sound the trumpets, everyone will know that evil has come upon them because of their evil deeds. . . . On the authority of the scribes, fasting is prescribed whenever trouble befalls a community until mercy is vouchsafed to it from heaven."

There are two distinct commandments: (1) There is a positive commandment of repentance and confession for any sin that a person commits. This commandment is set forth in Numbers 5:6–7, "When a man or a woman commits any sin . . . then they shall confess their sin which they have done," and Maimonides, in his *Book of Knowledge*, devoted an entire section, The Laws of Repentance, comprising ten chapters, to it. (2) There is a specific obligation of repentance during a time of trouble, as set forth in Numbers 10:9, "And when ye go forth to war in your land against the adversary that oppresseth you, then ye shall sound an alarm with the trumpets; and ye shall be remembered before the Lord your God." In terms of concrete practice, this obligation of repentance, on a scriptural level, assumes the form of sounding the trumpets, and on a scribal level, the form of fasting.

Essentially the obligation of repentance in time of trouble is connected with the suffering of the community, as the Mishnah very precisely states, "for every trouble that befalls a community—may it not happen!" (Ta'anit 19a), and as Maimonides emphasizes in the text we cited just above. However, the obligation of an individual in trouble to return to God also stems from this biblical passage. The fact that the halakhah accords recognition to a fast undertaken by an individual demonstrates that there is an obligation of repentance devolving upon the individual who finds himself in difficult circumstances. According to Maimonides, there is no such thing as a fast devoid of repentance. Maimonides, in Laws of Fast Days 1:9, states: "Just as a community must fast when in trouble, so an individual must fast when in trouble." Similarly, the baraita states: "Our rabbis have taught: If a city is surrounded by [hostile] Gentiles or threatened with inundation by a river, or if a ship is foundering in the sea, or if an individual is pursued by Gentiles or by robbers or by an evil spirit, [the alarm is sounded even on the Sabbath]" (Ta'anit 2b). [The bracketed phrase at the end of the quotation is the correct reading of the text, according to the Rif, Rambam, Rosh, Maharshah, and others. *Translator*.] In all of these instances, then, it is permitted to sound the alarm (only verbally) on the Sabbath. This is also the ruling of Maimonides, as set forth in Laws of Fast Days 1:6. It follows from this that the obligation to cry out applies equally to the individual and the community. And of what value is crying out, if the cry does not issue forth from a soul that repents its sins? (It is understood that there is no law to sound the alarm *with trumpets*, even on a weekday, for an individual in trouble. One sounds the alarm with trumpets only for trouble which befalls a community. There are many laws, both in chapter 3 of Mishnah Ta'anit and in chapter 2 of Maimonides' Laws of Fast Days, establishing the nature of communal trouble, and none of these laws includes the individual in trouble. The only point of the baraita cited above is that an individual in trouble may cry out [according to Maimonides' explanation] even on the Sabbath.)

The difference between the general commandment of repentance and the specific obligation of repentance in time of trouble exhausts itself in one detail. Repentance for a sin is bound up with knowledge of the sin. As long as an individual is not aware of having committed any sin, he has no obligation to repent. One cannot oblige a person to seek atonement without knowledge of a sin, as it is said, "or if his sin be known to him wherein he

hath sinned" (Leviticus 4:23). It is knowledge of a sin
that obliges a person to bring a sin-offering. The same
holds true for repentance. A person is not obliged to
repent for concealed sins but only for revealed sins.
However, in a time of trouble, the sufferer must examine his actions and search out his sins so that he may be
able to repent for them. The very fact of suffering indicates the presence of sin and it commands a person:
Find your sins and return to your Creator. This scruti-
nizing of one's deeds is a characteristic feature of the
obligation of repentance bound up with suffering. We
know that on fast days the courts would meet in session
and examine the actions of the townspeople. The
Talmud states: "In the morning of fast days there is a
public assembly . . . and they examine the affairs of the
town" (Megillah 30b). Similarly, Maimonides, in Laws
of Fast Days 1:17, sets it down as a firmly established
ruling that "on each fast day undertaken by a community beset by trouble, the court and the elders should
meet in session at the synagogue and examine the deeds
of the townspeople. . . . They should remove all of the
obstacles [to righteous living] provided by transgressors
and should carefully search and inquire of the extor-
tioners and other criminals," (See Eruvin 13b: "and now
that he [man] is created, let him scrutinize his [past]
actions; and there are those who say: "let him be careful
about his [future] actions!'"). This obligation to scrutinize one's actions refers to a time of trouble. It would
seem that the special commandment of repentance on
the Day of Atonement (as set forth by Maimonides in
Laws of Repentance 2:7, and by Rabbenu Jonah in *Gates
of Repentance* 2:14 and 4:17) also involves, according to
the ruling of the halakhah, a special requirement of
repentance for concealed sins and the obligation to scrutinize one's deeds in order to uncover and bring to the
surface the degrading underside of a person's life. In
this respect, the obligation of repentance on the Day of

Atonement is identical with the obligation of repentance in a time of suffering. And it is with reference to such occasions that the verse states: "Let us search and try our ways, and return to the Lord" (Lamentations 3:40). [Cf. *Shi'urim le-Zekher Abba Mari Z"L*, vol. 1 (Jerusalem, 1983), pp. 190–192. *Translator.*]

4. The following remarks are based on the talmudic discussion in Bava Batra 15a–b, which cites the views of several sages who differ as to when and in which generation Job lived.

5. Sanhedrin 94a.

6. See Maimonides, Laws of Kings and Their Wars 1:9 and the critical gloss of the Rabad ad loc. However, even Maimonides' view refers only to the situation as it existed once the kingship had been given to David and does not apply to any king who reigned before him. See 1 Samuel 13:13–14. Already, at that moment, the divesting of the kingship from Saul's descendants had begun. There, as well, Saul could have mended his sin through repentance.

7. This concept is expressed by Rava in Sanhedrin 72a: "Rava said: 'What is the reason for the [law of the thief] breaking into a house? Because it is certain that no man is inactive where his property is concerned. Therefore . . .'"

8. Maimonides, in Laws of the Temple 6:16, states almost explicitly that the fact that the second sanctification, wrought by Ezra, remains in effect for its time and for eternity is grounded in the same reason he uses to explain why the holiness of the Temple precincts was not nullified. Physical destruction cannot expel the divine presence from the heap of ruins. [Cf. P. Peli, ed., *'Al ha-Teshuvah* (Jerusalem, 1975), pp. 300–308; and *Shi'urim le-Zekher Abba Mari Z"L*, vol. 1, pp. 169–175. *Translator.*]

9. Judah Halevi, *Kuzari* 2:24.

10. See *Yalkut Shimoni* on Deuteronomy 29:11, s.v.

shalosh beritot; Berakhot 48b: "It [the Torah] was given with three covenants," and Rashi ad loc.

11. Genesis Rabbah 42:8.

12. See R. David Kimḥi, *Book of Roots,* s.v. *'im:* "This word refers to joining and cleaving. And the word *'am* [people] is derived from it because an assembly of individuals and their joining together with one another is termed an *'am* [people]." See, as well, Gesenius, *Hebrew Lexicon,* s.v. *'am.*

13. See Tosafot, Menaḥot 37a, s.v. *O kum gali;* and *Shitah Mekubbezet* ad loc., par. 18.

14. Sotah 37b; Sanhedrin 43b; and Rashi on Deuteronomy 29:28.

15. See Maimonides, Laws of the Foundations of the Torah 5:11.

16. Maimonides, Laws of Gifts to the Poor 10:2.

17. The talmudic opinion that "the Holy One, blessed be He, overturned the mountain upon them like an [inverted] cask" (Shabbat 88a) expresses the idea that the Almighty suggested to the Israelites that they accept the Torah and devote themselves to Him of their own freewill in order, thereby, to live as a holy nation, instead of living an involuntary, fate-laden existence that might be compared to having a mountain overturned upon one like an inverted cask. See Tosafot ad loc., s.v. *kafah* and *moda'ah.* [See "The Lonely Man of Faith," *Tradition* (Summer, 1965), p. 28, note **, for a different approach. *Translator.*]

18. See R. Jonah ibn Janaḥ, *Book of Roots* (translated from the Arabic into Hebrew by R. Judah ibn Tibbon and edited by Wilhelm Bacher, Berlin, 1896), s.v. *goy.* See, as well, R. David Kimḥi, *Book of Roots,* s.v. *goy:* "R. Jonah [ibn Janaḥ] states that the word *goy* can refer to an individual: for example, in the verse 'Wilt Thou slay a person [*goy*] even if he be righteous?' (Genesis 20:4)." [See *Sefer ha-Rikmah,* translated from the Arabic into Hebrew by R. Judah ibn Tibbon and edited by Michael

Wilenski (Berlin, 1929), chap. 28 (27), p. 307. *Translator*.]
See also Solomon Mandelkorn, *Concordance*, s.v. *goy*: "It
refers to individuals, members of one people, who have
become, as it were, one body." See, as well, Gesenius,
Hebrew Lexicon, s.v. *goy*. There are times, however, when
we find the word *goy* used to describe a herd of animals:
for example, "For a nation (*goy*) is come up upon my
land" (Joel 1:6, referring to a plague of locusts). It is
understood that in referring to animals the word is
being used in a derivative sense. See Radak and Rashi
ad loc. See, as well, the commentary of the Gaon of Vilna
to Isaiah 1:4, "Ah, sinful nation, a people laden with
iniquity," where the Gaon states: "The word '*am* refers
to a group of many people, a multitude . . . while the
word *goy* refers to those who adhere to a code of behavior. . . . And this is what our sages said [in the
Haggadah] in commenting on the verse 'And he became
there a great . . . nation' (Deuteronomy 26:5): 'This
teaches that the Israelites were distinctive there.'"

19. The phrase "a holy people" ('*am kadosh*) signifies
a community that has elevated its peoplehood to the
rank of holiness; it is, therefore, identical in meaning
with the term "holy nation" (*goy kadosh*).

20. Jewish uniqueness began to be forged in the
Egyptian crucible of affliction. This historical suffering
fashioned the image of the community as a nation possessing a distinctive character and its own individual
countenance, and, thereby, prepared it for that great
and exalted moment when God made a covenant of destiny with it at Sinai. The verse "The Aramean [Laban]
sought to destroy my father [Jacob], and he [Jacob] went
down into Egypt, and he became there a great . . .
nation" (Deuteronomy 26:5) testifies to the birth of
Jewish uniqueness in Egypt. How fine is the interpretation of this verse offered by our sages: "This teaches that
the Israelites were distinctive there." Nationhood and
distinctiveness as a special well-defined entity are one

and the same. In truth, the entire purpose of the bondage in Egypt was to create this people-nation of Israel. The Israelites went down into Egypt as the sons of Jacob but went up from there as a people bound to God and as a nation ready for the revelation of the divine presence and for God's making a covenant of destiny with them at Sinai. "When God wanted to make his [Abraham's] descendants a unique people, a perfect people, and to draw them near to Him, had they not first gone down into Egypt and been refined there, they would not have been His special people" (*Zohar* I, 83a). "However, until they went down into Egypt they were not yet a nation. . . . It is written, 'as a rose among the thorns, so is my love among the daughters' (Song of Songs 2:2). The Holy One, blessed be He, desired to make Israel according to the supernal pattern, so that there should be one rose on earth, even as it is on high. Now the rose that gives out a sweet aroma and is conspicuous among all other roses is the one that grows among the thorns" (*Zohar* II, 189b).

21 . A congregation can also signify devotion to a destructive ideology by individuals who are plotting evil: for example, "this evil congregation" (Numbers 14:35) and "that he fare not as Korah and his congregation" (Numbers 17:5).

22. See Maimonides, Laws of Repentance 3:11. "One who separates himself from the ways of the community, even if he does not commit transgressions, but disassociates himself from the congregation of Israel and does not perform commandments in their midst and does not share in their troubles and does not observe their fasts, but goes his own way as one of the Gentiles and as if he were not one of them—such a person has no share in the world-to-come."

23. Maimonides, Laws of Forbidden Intercourse 13:1–3, basing himself upon the baraita in Keritot 9a, states clearly that there was no immersion in Egypt and

conversion took effect through circumcision alone, and
that it was at Sinai that the Jews were commanded for
the first time to immerse themselves in order to undergo conversion. Maimonides states: "Israel entered into
the covenant by way of three rites—circumcision,
immersion, and sacrifice. Circumcision took place in
Egypt, as it is said, 'but no uncircumcised person shall
eat thereof' (Exodus 12:48). Our master, Moses, circumcised the people. . . . Immersion took place in the wilderness before the revelation of the Torah, as it is said, 'and
sanctify them today and tomorrow, and let them wash
their garments'" (Exodus 19:10). Maimonides explains
the statement in the sugya in Yevamot 71a ("But in truth
[the text 'A sojourner and a hired servant shall not eat
thereof' (Exodus 12:45)] comes to include a convert who
was circumcised but did not immerse himself") as referring to the Passover offering in all generations subse-
quent to the Exodus but not to the Passover celebrated
in Egypt itself, for in Egypt, according to all opinions,
conversion was effected, fully and completely, by circumcision alone. Similarly, Maimonides interprets the
statement of R. Joshua in Yevamot 46b ("Our forefathers
also underwent immersion") as referring to immersion
at the time of the revelation of the Torah, as the plain
meaning of the verses cited in the sugya seems to indicate. However, Maimonides would admit that the
"mothers," i.e., the women, immersed themselves even
in Egypt, as stated clearly in the sugya there. For one
cannot say that the women immersed themselves only
prior to the revelation of the Torah and not in Egypt.
Such an assertion would run up against an insuperable
objection, already raised and emphasized by Rashi in
his commentary ad loc., s.v. be-imahot: "And their wives
immersed themselves, as the gemara explains later on;
for if they did not immerse themselves, then through
what [act] did they enter under the wings of the divine
presence?" To paraphrase Rashi, some act is required

for conversion to be effected. Similarly, the Tosefta, Pesaḥim 8:18, states that those handmaidens in Egypt who did not immerse themselves could not eat of the Passover offering. This holds true according to the first anonymous tannaitic view cited in the Tosefta as well as according to the view of R. Eliezer b. Yaakov. See Rabad, critical gloss to Maimonides, Laws of the Passover Offering 5:5. In truth, we could claim that even the males immersed themselves in Egypt, in addition to being circumcised, and that at Sinai they were commanded to undergo a new, second immersion necessitated by the revelation of the Torah, which conferred an added measure of holiness upon them. According to this view, every act of conversion, including the conversion which took place in Egypt, requires immersion. In support of this view, one may adduce the position of many *Rishonim*, including Maimonides (Laws of Forbidden Intercourse 13:12), that the second immersion of a slave—the immersion after he has been freed—is a scriptural requirement, inasmuch as he is acquiring an added measure of holiness, and now, as a free person, is attaining the complete measure of the holiness of Israel. It is understandable, then, that the Jews at Sinai, upon entering into the covenant of the Torah and the commandments, required an additional immersion, over and above the immersion that had taken place in Egypt. One could argue that even the *Nimmukei Yosef* [see *Nimmukei Yosef* on the Rif, Yevamot 16b, s.v. *kiddushav kiddushin*], who states that the immersion of the slave after he has been freed is only a rabbinic requirement, would concede that the Israelites were required to immerse themselves at Sinai. One can distinguish between the case of the slave who already [upon becoming a slave] had been converted through circumcision and immersion, and via these rites had entered into the covenant, and the case of the Israelites at Sinai, who had to acquire an added measure of holiness, since they were entering into a second covenant. With reference to a slave, the view of the *Nimmukei Yosef* is that his being emancipated does not confer an additional measure of holiness upon him but, rather, removes a legal impediment. The slave's holiness is complete upon his undergoing circumcision and immersion. However, as long as he is a slave his servitude prevents him from being obliged to observe the positive time-bound commandments and forbids him to marry an Israelite woman. However, if the servitude is nullified through his being set free, then he is lacking nothing. It is for this reason that there is no scriptural requirement of immersion upon his emancipation. However, the Israelites at Sinai acquired a new level of holiness, a level of holiness that did not exist beforehand. Therefore, they required a second conversion rite and consequently a second immersion.

One may ask: Why didn't the Israelites require the symbolic letting of the blood of the covenant (*hatafat dam berit*) at Sinai as well? The following answer may be suggested. Circumcision, which always precedes immersion and by itself does not confer the holiness of Israel upon an individual, need not be undergone a second time (through the symbolic letting of the blood) when an additional measure of holiness is conferred upon a person. All we require is that an individual have had a proper circumcision for the sake of conversion; and if such a circumcision took place, then, even though at that time he only attained a lesser measure of holiness, he need not undergo the symbolic letting of blood when he attains a greater measure of holiness. Similarly, the slave who is freed does not undergo the symbolic letting of blood, even though he is now obliged to perform new commandments and is acquiring a greater measure of holiness, inasmuch as, to begin with, he underwent a proper circumcision for the sake of the conversion of servitude. However, immersion, which completes the act of conversion and gives rise to the holiness of Israel, has to be undergone a second time when the convert ascends from a lesser level of holiness to a greater level.

We are, however, confronted with a problem on examining the view of Naḥmanides. Naḥmanides, in his *Hiddushim* (Novellae) on Yevamot 47b, s.v. *nitrapeh*, states that if a convert first immersed himself and then was circumcised, the conversion is valid. According to this view, then, there can be times when circumcision comes at the conclusion of the conversion process. If that is so, we should reverse matters and require the symbolic letting of blood and not immersion in a case where the person is acquiring a greater measure of holiness.

In order to answer this problem we must examine another statement of Naḥmanides. In his *Hiddushim* on Yevamot 46a, s.v. *sheken maẓinu*, Naḥmanides is of the view that the Levites, who had been circumcised prior to the Exodus for the sake of fulfilling the commandments and not for the sake of conversion, did not require the symbolic letting of blood. Naḥmanides states: "This being so [that the Levites had been circumcised beforehand], how did they enter under the wings of the divine presence? But they underwent the symbolic letting of blood. It would appear to me, however, that in terms of the law requiring circumcision [for the purpose of conversion], the Levites did not require the symbolic letting of blood, for they were already circumcised. Nor may they be compared to a circumcised Arab or a circumcised Gibeonite [who does require the symbolic letting of blood if he is being converted]. For since he [the Arab or the Gibeonite] never received a command of circumcision, it is as if he is not circumcised at all." It is clear from Naḥmanides' statement that circumcision, unlike immersion, is not an integral part of the conversion process. Rather, its purpose is to divest the convert of his status as an 'arel (one who is uncircumcised). If the convert was not circumcised, he cannot acquire the holiness of Israel, for a person who is an 'arel cannot enter into the covenant. Therefore, if a person is converting and he has already been circumcised, he can [forgo the symbolic letting of blood and] immerse himself for the purpose of conversion. A circumcised Arab, since he was not circumcised for the purpose of conversion, is regarded as an 'arel, as is stated in Nedarim 31b, Yevamot 71a, and Avodah Zarah 27a. Therefore, when he converts he must undergo the symbolic letting of blood. However, the Levites, who were descendants of Abraham and were circumcised in accordance with God's commandment to their father Abraham, did not require the symbolic letting of blood.

In light of this premise we may now answer our question as to why, according to Nahmanides who is of the opinion that at times conversion is concluded by the act of circumcision, we should not require circumcision [or, to be more precise, the symbolic letting of blood] for the sake of acquiring a greater measure of holiness.

We have seen that circumcision does not really belong to the conversion procedure; its whole purpose is exhausted in divesting a person of his status as an 'arel. It is for this reason that a person who is already circumcised and is consequently not an 'arel need not undergo the symbolic letting of blood when he ascends from a lesser level of holiness to a greater level. Immersion differs fundamentally from circumcision, for immersion is an act which gives rise to the holiness of Israel and constitutes an integral part of the conversion procedure. Therefore, in order for a person to acquire a greater measure of holiness, immersion is required, but not the symbolic letting of blood. Nahmanides, however, [despite his agreement with the above] is of the opinion that immersion can take place before circumcision, for even though the convert does not become an

Israelite immediately upon emerging from his immersion, the immersion, nevertheless, is effective for the future. Once he is circumcised and not an *'arel*, the immersion that took place prior to the circumcision effects the conversion and gives rise to his status as an Israelite.

The question as to whether circumcision is part of the conversion procedure or whether it serves only to divest the Gentile of his status as an *'arel*, which status interposes between him and the holiness of Israel, is dependent on a dispute between the *Rishonim* as to whether the presence of a court is required when the convert is undergoing circumcision.

From certain statements of Maimonides (Laws of Forbidden Intercourse 13:6, 14:5–6), it would appear that his view is that the presence of a court is required only for immersion. Therefore, it would seem that according to Maimonides, circumcision serves only to remove the Gentile's status as an *'arel*, which status serves as a legal impediment to conversion. [The presence of a court is required for the conversion procedure. Since a court is not required for circumcision, it is evidently not part of the conversion procedure. *Translator*.]

The *Tur* (Yoreh De'ah: Laws of Converts 268) and the Shulḥan Arukh (Yoreh De'ah: Laws of Converts 268:3), on the other hand, require the presence of a court for circumcision as well as for immersion. [This would indicate that circumcision is part of the conversion procedure. *Translator*.] Moreover, the very same view is set forth explicitly by Naḥmanides in his *Ḥiddushim* on Yevamot 45b, s.v. *mi lo tavlah*. This would appear to controvert our assumption that the sole purpose of circumcision, according to Naḥmanides, is to divest the convert of his status as an *'arel*. The very fact that Naḥmanides requires the presence of a court during circumcision indicates that the act of circumcision is an act which effects conversion and therefore must be an act of the court. Our original question arises anew. Why didn't the Levites undergo the symbolic letting of blood at Sinai since their circumcision, to begin with, was not undergone for the sake of conversion? (To be sure, Naḥmanides in his *Ḥiddushim* on Yevamot 45b, s.v. *mi lo*, agrees with the view of the Tosafot, Yevamot 45b, s.v. *mi lo*, that immersion and circumcision, if done for the sake of performing a commandment, are sufficient [for conversion, even if they were not performed for the sake of conversion]. In support of his view, Naḥmanides cites a statement from the Palestinian Talmud, Kiddushin 3:12. However, this view of Naḥmanides would still not serve to resolve our problem. Circumcision and immersion for the sake of performing a commandment can qualify as valid elements in the conversion procedure only after the laws of conversion were revealed and the ruling was established that conversion takes place through circumcision and immersion. In such a context, circumcision and immersion effect conversion even if they were done for the sake of performing commandments and not for the sake of conversion. Included in the intent of the commandment is the commandment as an act effecting conversion. However, the Levites were circumcised in Egypt before the Israelites were commanded to circumcise themselves for the purpose of conversion, of entering under the wings of the divine presence. This being the case, their circumcision could not have constituted an act of conversion, since the Israelites were only charged with circumcision for the sake of conversion afterwards.)

It would appear that Naḥmanides is of the opinion that circumcision constitutes an integral part of the conversion procedure only as long as the convert has not already performed the commandment of circumcision properly. But once he has performed the commandment, it would not be part of the procedure.

Circumcision, as an act of conversion, takes effect only when the individual is lacking in the performance of the commandment of circumcision. Therefore, a circumcised Arab who converts requires the symbolic letting of blood because his circumcision is of no value, and through the symbolic letting of blood he will fulfill the commandment of entering into the covenant of our father Abraham, which is an inextricable part of the commandment of circumcision. However, the Levites, as descendants of Abraham, had already fulfilled the commandment of circumcision in all its fine details, and had completely discharged their obligation. Therefore, they did not require the symbolic letting of blood. For what would they accomplish thereby? It follows that their conversion was effected by immersion alone, as is the case with women or with one whose male organ has been cut off. Thus Naḥmanides, at the conclusion of his discussion of the Levites, states: "Therefore, the Levites are adjudged as women, so that they would enter under the wings of the divine presence through immersion." Therefore, when a convert ascends from a lesser to a greater holiness he does not require the symbolic letting of blood, for he completely fulfilled the commandment of circumcision previously. In contrast to circumcision, immersion is part of the conversion procedure not because one is fulfilling a commandment or discharging an obligation through its performance. For immersion, aside from its significance as an act effecting conversion, does not constitute any type of legal performance. Therefore, immersion, in terms of its conferring upon one the holiness of Israel, can be undergone many times, and every time one acquires a greater measure of holiness, one requires immersion.

24. That the acceptance of the yoke of the commandments accompanies immersion, inasmuch as immersion gives rise to the status of one's being an Israelite, is almost a truism. This view is set forth in the sugya in

Yevamot 47a–b and seems to be implied as well by Maimonides' statements in Laws of Forbidden Intercourse 13:12 and 14:6 (the latter ruling being based on the above sugya). Rashi, in his commentary on the sugya, s.v. *u-modi'in oto*, makes the point explicitly: "Since he acquires the status of a convert through immersion, therefore, when he undergoes the obligatory immersion he must accept upon himself the yoke of commandments." However, the Tosafot, Yevamot 45b, s.v. *mi lo tavlah*, states that the acceptance of the yoke of the commandments can precede immersion.

Maimonides, in Laws of Forbidden Intercourse 13:17, states: "A convert who was not examined or who was not informed about the commandments and the punishments [for transgressing them], but was circumcised and immersed in the presence of three laymen, is deemed a [valid] convert." I once heard from my father and master [R. Moses Soloveitchik] of blessed memory, that Maimonides does not mean to say that a person who converted with the intention of not observing the commandments is deemed a valid convert. Such a notion would subvert the entire concept of conversion and the holiness of Israel, which exhausts itself in our obligation to fulfill God's commandments. Maimonides' position is that the acceptance of the commandments, unlike immersion, does not constitute a distinct act in the process of conversion that would require the presence of a court. Rather, acceptance of the commandments is a defining feature of the conversion process that must be undergone for the sake of fulfilling the commandments. Therefore, if we know that the convert, at the time of immersion, is willing to accept the yoke of the commandments, the immersion effects conversion even though there was no special act of informing the convert about the commandments and his consenting to fulfill them, since the convert intends to live the holy life of an observant Jew. It would appear, however, that the

view of the Tosafot, cited earlier, is that the acceptance
of the commandments is a distinct element in the conversion process and, consequently, that the law necessi-
tating the presence of a court refers to the court's presence at the act of acceptance. Only this act of acceptance—and not immersion—requires the presence of the
court.

Nahmanides, in his *Hiddushim* on Yevamot 45b, s.v.
mi lo tavlah, states: "Even a male convert who accepted
[the commandments] upon himself prior to his being
circumcised must once again accept [them] upon himself when he immerses himself." It would seem, at first
glance, that according to Nahmanides there is an act of
acceptance of the commandments which takes place at
the time of circumcision. However, one might suggest
that Nahmanides is not referring to a special act of
acceptance of the commandments at the time of circumcision, but, rather, is characterizing the general nature of
circumcision. Circumcision must be undergone for the
sake of obligating oneself to fulfill the commandments.
This interpretation of Nahmanides' view is similar to
the explanation offered earlier with respect to
Maimonides' position. Maimonides, however, is of the
opinion that the absence of a distinct act of acceptance of
the commandments does not constitute any legal
impediment to the validity of the conversion.
Nahmanides, on the other hand, agrees with the Tosafot
that there is a distinct act of acceptance of the commandments and that it requires the presence of a court.
However, Nahmanides believes that aside from the distinct act of acceptance, both circumcision and immersion must be undergone for the sake of being obliged to
perform the commandments, that is to say, for the sake
of conversion.

25. Maimonides, Laws of Kings and Their Wars 5:4,
writes the following regarding the seven nations of
Canaan: "It is a positive commandment to destroy the

seven nations, as it is said: 'But thou shalt utterly destroy them' (Deuteronomy 20:17). If one does not kill any of them that falls into one's power, one transgresses a negative commandment, as it is said: 'Thou shalt save nothing that breatheth' (Deuteronomy 20:16). But their memory has long since perished." The Radbaz, in his commentary ad loc., notes that the source for Maimonides' concluding comment, "But their memory has long since perished," is the statement of Rabbi Joshua in Mishnah Yadayim 4:4: "Sennacherib, king of Assyria, came up and intermingled all the peoples."

It is, however, striking and passing strange that Maimonides, in setting forth the commandment to wipe out Amalek, does not add the concluding phrase, "But their memory has long since perished." Thus states Maimonides in Laws of Kings and Their Wars 5:5: "Similarly it is a positive commandment to destroy the remembrance of Amalek, as it is said: 'Thou shalt blot out the remembrance of Amalek' (Deuteronomy 25:19). It is also a positive commandment to remember always his evil deeds and the waylaying [he resorted to], so that we keep afresh the hatred manifested by him, as it is said: 'Remember what Amalek did unto thee' (Deuteronomy 25:17). The traditional interpretation of this injunction is: 'Remember,' by word of mouth; 'Do not forget,' out of mind, that it is forbidden to forget his hatred and enmity." It would appear from Maimonides' statements that Amalek is still in existence, while the seven nations have descended into the abyss of oblivion.

One may query: Why didn't Maimonides apply R. Joshua's principle that "Sennacherib, king of Assyria, came up and intermingled all the peoples" to Amalek as he did to the seven nations? The answer to this question is very simple. Scripture testifies that Amalek is still in existence. Note what the Torah states: "The Lord will have war with Amalek from generation to generation"

(Exodus 17:16). If that is the case, then it is impossible that Amalek be completely destroyed before the coming of the Messiah. As the sages state: "The [divine] throne will not be whole and the [divine] Name will not be whole until the descendants of Amalek are completely blotted out" (Midrash Tanḥuma on Ki Teẓe, end; and Rashi on Exodus 17:16). But—where is he? I once heard the following answer from my father and master [R. Moses Soloveitchik] of blessed memory, namely, that any nation that conspires to destroy Keneset Israel becomes, according to the halakhah, Amalek. My father and master added: We have been charged with two commandments concerning Amalek. The first is the obligation to blot out his memory. This obligation devolves upon every person with reference to an individual Amalekite and is set forth in the verse "Thou shall blot out the remembrance of Amalek" (Deuteronomy 25:19). The second is the readiness to do battle as a community against the people Amalek. This requirement is set forth in the verse, "The Lord will have war with Amalek from generation to generation" (Exodus 17:16). Thus, if any people seeks to destroy us, we are commanded to do battle against it when it rises up against us, and this battle of ours is an obligatory war (*milḥemet miẓvah*) on the basis of the verse from Exodus, "The Lord will have war with Amalek from generation to generation." However, the obligation to wipe out individual Amalekites, as set forth in the verse from Deuteronomy, applies only to genealogical descendants of Amalek. Now it is true that Maimonides' ruling also includes the obligation to blot out individuals, an obligation which does not apply to any nation other than Amalek, even if that nation seeks to destroy the Jewish people [and this obligation is no longer in force, since there are no longer any identifiable genealogical descendants of Amalek]. Nevertheless, since the obligation to do battle against Amalek as a